The Stranger's Long Neck

The Stranger's Long Neck

How to Deliver What Your Customers Really Want Online

Gerry McGovern

A & C Black • London

First published in Great Britain 2010, reprinted 2011

A & C Black Publishers Ltd
36 Soho Square, London W1D 3QY
www.acblack.com

A CIP record for this book is available from the British Library.

ISBN: 9-781-4081-1442-1

This book is produced using paper that is made from wood grown
in managed, sustainable forests. It is natural, renewable and
recyclable. The logging and manufacturing processes conform to
the environmental regulations of the country of origin.

Design by Fiona Pike, Pike Design, Winchester
Typeset by Saxon Graphics Ltd, Derby
Printed in Spain by GraphyCems

Contents

Acknowledgements

This book would not be possible without the support and collaboration of a wide range of people and organizations. I have been lucky to work with a lot of great people over the years.

Firstly, I'd like to thank those who generously gave of their time and expertise to read and comment on early drafts, including Fredrik Wackå, Gord Hopkins, Eirik Rønjum, Ove Dalen, and Scott Smith. They managed to identify problems and the book is significantly improved because of their input.

Much of this book is based on my experience working with a wide variety of organizations. I'd particularly like to thank Microsoft. Although I live in Dublin I have so much interaction with Microsoft that sometimes I feel like I live in Seattle. I've learned a lot from Microsoft and would particularly like to thank Suzanne Sowinska, Alex Blanton, Peter Horsman, Laurel Hale, Meyyammai Subramanian, Katherine Inman, and Jason Kozleski.

Another organization that requires special thanks is Tetra Pak who has been extremely generous to me over the years. I'd particularly like to thank Jenny Almstrom who always brings great enthusiasm and energy to her work. Gabriel Olsson deserves special mention too, and I owe my sincere thanks to Nancy Helledie and Jörgen Haglind for kindly approving the Tetra Pak case study.

I would also like to thank Enterprise Ireland, Scottish Enterprise, Innovation Norway, NHS Choices, Cisco, and OECD (thanks Cynthia!).

I'd like to thank Alison O'Byrne for proofreading the manuscript, and also my son Aonghus for his excellent editing and general research help.

There are many, many inspiring figures out there when it comes to putting the customer at the center of the web universe, but here are a few that have particularly inspired me over the years: Jared Spool, Jakob Nielsen, and Seth Godin.

chapter 1

Trading with strangers

If life is a competitive struggle, why is there so much cooperation about? And why, in particular, are people such eager cooperators…The thing that needs explaining about human beings is not their frequent vice, but their occasional virtue.

Matt Ridley

DESIGNING WEB SITES FOR STRANGERS

The man who had suddenly appeared at the top of the hill was a stranger. Right below him, and carrying a dead boar between them, were three men who had hunted in this area since childhood. Fear flicked across the stranger's face. His nostrils flared as he sucked in more air; his eyes widened, and the landscape became larger before him. The three men dropped the boar and raised their weapons.

They stood there, staring at each other. The stranger tried his best to smile. Two of the men glanced at their leader for a sign. Then the sun came out. The chain of colorful stones the stranger was wearing around his neck glistened and sparkled.

If there's one reason more than any other that Web sites fail, it's because the web teams managing them lack understanding of, and empathy for, their customers.

The leader's eyes focused on the stones and he now wore an inquisitive expression. He had never seen such beautiful stones before. Then something amazing happened. Instead of killing the stranger and taking his colorful stones, he decided to trade. He would offer the hungry stranger some of his boar in exchange for those fantastic stones.

Somewhere in the not too distant past, trade between strangers began. The old way had been "fight or flight". If you saw strangers, you either ran from them or tried to kill them. Once we learned to trade with strangers, our world jumped on a rollercoaster of change and progress. We ventured beyond our tight-knit families and tribes to build cities and civilizations. We moved from isolated villages to the global village, and to the World Wide Web.

If there's one reason more than any other that Web sites fail, it's because the web teams managing them lack understanding of, and empathy for, their customers. The customer is a stranger and this book is about helping you understand your customers so that you can create more intuitive Web sites that are truly easy to use.

The pull of the tribe—the organization or departmental unit—is great, but it is the single greatest source of Web site failure. This book will give you a range of techniques to avoid that pull and to truly understand and design for the stranger. And it is as much about intranets as it is about public Web sites. Remember, employees are the customers of the intranet.

To live in the modern world is to be surrounded by strangers. To live in the primitive world is to live only with family, the department, the tribe of graphic designers, or content writers. This you must resist, which will be hard because the Web is a cold place. It's not like running a shop or a restaurant or an office. You don't get the normal feedback you would get if you were a manager and walked into your supermarket and saw big queues at the checkouts or unhappy faces.

Real people use your Web site every day. Real people? Yes, real people. Strange as it may seem, that's an incredibly hard thing for most of us involved in Web site management to understand. And out of sight is out of mind. We don't see these "people", so in essence they don't exist. That is why Web sites fail. The Web sites that succeed get constant feedback from their customers as they seek to complete tasks on the Web site.

This book gives you methods to get that feedback in the form of defensible management metrics. Over a 15-year period, the ideas have been developed within some of the world's largest organizations, including Microsoft, Tetra Pak, Rolls-Royce, Schlumberger, IKEA, Cisco, and OECD (Organization for Economic Co-Operation and Development).

The essential underlying method is called task management, which is based on the following principles:

1. **Every Web site has a small set of tasks that deliver a huge amount of value. These are the top tasks and they exist in what I call the Long Neck.**

2. **Every Web site has a large range of tiny tasks. Carefully managed, these tasks have the potential to deliver value, but they also have real potential to destroy value by getting in the way of the top tasks.**

3. **Manage the top tasks, not the content or the technology. Focus relentlessly on helping your customers complete the top tasks as quickly and easily as possible.**

You need to think like your customer and use the words your customers use.

THE EARTHWORM AND THE HUMAN

There are two skills you must develop if you want to succeed in web management. The first is empathy for your customer. You have to develop a real feeling for your customer (the stranger), to think like your customer and use the words your customer uses. Easy to say, but one of the most difficult challenges that any of us faces is walking in someone else's shoes.

The second skill involves linking and connecting. The Web is, in essence, a network and you must combine empathy for your customers with an understanding of the journey they are on—the tasks they need to complete. In order for them to complete their tasks you will have to create appropriate links. Linking seems simple, but is incredibly hard to do right, because to create great links you must be truly thinking like your customer, using their language, making it as simple as possible for them, and saving them as much time as possible.

When researchers finally counted the number of genes in the human body, they were a bit depressed. They had expected to find a lot more. You see, they already knew that an earthworm has about 20,000 unique genes. Surely, the grand and majestic human would have at least 10 times more?

Not so. The poor old human only possesses about 30,000 unique genes. (Now the earthworms were delighted. It was front-page news on *Earthworm Daily*, and they partied for a week.)

Both humans and earthworms are networks. And a network is made up of two things. There is the node, the gene, the webpage. This is the place, the thing, the entity. But the gene on its own is not a network. It needs something else that is much more crucial in creating a network. So what is it that makes a network a network?

It is the link, the connection. And this is the difference, a major difference, between us and those party-animal earthworms.

Humans, you see, may not have all that many more genes than an earthworm, but we have far more links between our genes. It is the connections between our genes that makes us human, and it is the lack of connections between earthworm genes that makes earthworms, earthworms. So, even at the genetic level, there is a simple and compelling message: It pays to connect, it pays to link, it pays to cooperate.

What about *The Selfish Gene*, you might justifiably ask? That wonderful book by Richard Dawkins brilliantly made the case that all genes care about is perpetuating themselves, and they use us humans and other species simply as gene-carriers and gene-replicating machines.

Maybe so, but Dawkins points out that even the selfish gene has learned to cooperate:

Colonies of genes they may be but, in their behavior, bodies have undeniably acquired an individuality of their own. An animal moves as a coordinated whole, as a unit. Subjectively, I feel like a unit, not a colony. This is to be expected. Selection has favored genes that cooperate with others. In the fierce competition for scarce resources, in the relentless struggle to eat other survival machines, and to avoid being eaten, there must have been a premium on central coordination rather than anarchy within the communal body.

Linking is what makes the Web, the Web. Over the years, through a whole range of customer tests, I have found that there are three things that really annoy customers when they visit a Web site:

- **confusing menus and links**
- **poor search results**
- **out-of-date information**

THE PARETO PRINCIPLE – STRETCHED

According to Wikipedia, "The Pareto principle states that, for many events, 80% of the effects come from 20% of the causes."

Vilfredo Pareto was an Italian economist and sociologist. He noticed that 80% of Italy's wealth was owned by 20% of Italians and when he surveyed other countries he found that the same principle applied. Through continuous research on Web sites over an eight-year period in 15 countries with over 60,000 test participants on a wide range of subjects, we (my associates and I) have found that:

- **25% of effects come from 5% of causes;**
- **60% (not 80% as Pareto suggests) of effects come from 20% of causes.**

What does this mean? A very small set of things (the Long Neck) has a huge impact—5% of things have 25% of the influence. On every Web site there is a small set of super-important tasks that your customers wish to complete. You must get these tasks right, otherwise you lose your customers. We have found that this Long Neck phenomenon occurs when people are using Web sites to decide:

- **what they want from a vacation destination;**
- **what is important to them from a personal development point of view;**

- **what they want from a new car;**
- **how they are going to choose a university;**
- **how they search on the Web to find out more about Barack Obama or John McCain, etc.**

Much of the Long Tail is a Dead Zone. It's a dead and useless tail full of dead and useless content.

THE PROBLEM WITH THE LONG TAIL

One of the key promises of the Web is the collapse of geography. We can go all over the world in an instant. And we can buy and sell digital items at almost zero distribution and storage cost. Physical things that used to be difficult to locate are now much easier to find.

In 2004, Chris Anderson, editor of *Wired* magazine, coined the term "Long Tail". According to Anderson:

The theory of the Long Tail is that our culture and economy are increasingly shifting away from a focus on a relatively small number of "hits" (mainstream products and markets) at the head of the demand curve and toward a huge number of niches in the tail. As the costs of production and distribution fall, especially online, there is now less need to lump products and consumers into one-size-fits-all containers. In an era without the constraints of physical shelf space and other bottlenecks of distribution, narrowly-targeted goods and services can be as economically attractive as mainstream fare.

The Long Tail is a great concept and is definitely true in many situations. Being a fan of somewhat obscure music, I'm certainly delighted that I can use the Web to get music I would otherwise have been unable to find.

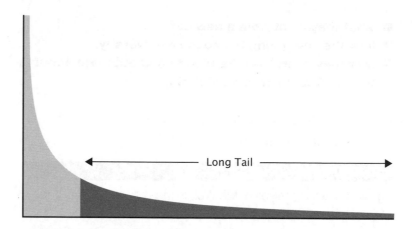

A problem with the Long Tail theory is that it is primarily concerned with the costs of storage and distribution, which, it points out, are negligible for digital content. There are other costs, including:

● **creation**
● **finding**
● **review**

Creation

We are now told that content will be created for free by a bunch of enthusiastic amateurs. In certain cases this is true, in other cases not. It's hard to see a bunch of enthusiastic amateurs producing animation films of the same quality as Pixar's, or creating blockbusters like *Avatar*.

While there has been an explosion in writing for children, it is not evident that there has been an explosion of J. K. Rowlings. It's very easy to make and distribute music, but it's not so easy to find the new Beatles, Rolling Stones, Bob Dylan, or Velvet Underground. Have you used an intranet that employs the enthusiastic amateur content development model? It doesn't work very well, does it?

There is a book inside everybody and the Web lets that book out. Quality content does not increase just because you increase the amount of content created. It just becomes harder to find.

Finding

Every time you add a piece of content to your Web site you affect:

- **the quality of the navigation;**
- **the quality of the search;**
- **your ability to manage the content on an ongoing basis.**

Every piece of content requires at least one link, and sometimes many more. The fewer links you have, the less likely they are to be confusing. (Of course, too few links and you're into earthworm territory.)

It's easier to manage a quality search environment for a Web site with 1,000 pages than one with 10,000. It's simply more likely that the right result will come first. A good search engine is less than half the battle. Managing a quality search environment is more about psychology than technology. It's about understanding the words people use and why they use them. Just because someone searches for "cheap hotel" does not necessarily mean they want a cheap hotel. Perhaps what they're really after is a four-star hotel at a two-star price?

Review

Certain types of content don't require ongoing review to ensure they are maintaining their quality. Much art, music, and literature can't be wrong, so to speak. However, a description of how to treat a particular disease can become wrong as a result of new research. Product details may need updating, telephone numbers may change, policies and procedures may become outdated. In other words, some content goes out of date, and that is a significant cost of Web site management.

Most web teams have a culture of launch-and-leave, when what they really need is a culture of review-and-remove and a continuous improvement of top tasks. That's a cost—and the bigger the Web site, the bigger the cost.

Entering the Dead Zone

Much of the Long Tail is a Dead Zone. It's a dead and useless tail full of dead and useless content. Perhaps it would be manageable if this dead and useless content stayed in the tail. Unfortunately, it doesn't. It confuses the link options and gets found in search results, disguised as useful content by including words that people search for when they're looking to complete top tasks.

Because people are so impatient, they often don't notice and end up using this useless content. They follow instructions that were intended for a previous version of the product. They take down the wrong number, they think the training event is on July 10, when that July 10 was for the previous year, and so on.

This sort of content is not just low value, it's destructive to value. Later, you'll find out how to measure the impact of this destruction of value which undermines credibility, brand, and trust. We call it a "disaster" when customers come to your Web site and think they've gotten the right information when in fact it's wrong.

In an age when there has never been as much stuff thrown at us, it's never been more important to understand the essence of the situation.

THE LONG NECK

This book is about the other end of the graph, how to keep the Dead Zone content at bay. Sometimes this top end is referred to as the "head". Through analysis of hundreds of such graphs it occurred to me that the "head" really looks more like a neck.

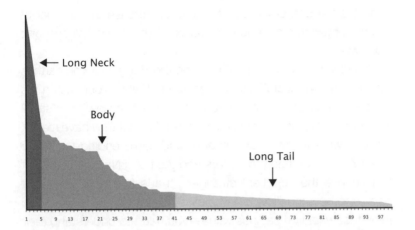

I began to notice three distinct sections of the graph:

- **Long Neck:** Roughly 5% of the content accounts for 25% of the demand;
- **Body:** 35% or so of the content accounts for about 55% of the demand;
- **Long Tail and Dead Zone:** 60% of the content accounts for about 20% of the demand.

In an age when there has never been as much stuff thrown at us, it's never been more important to understand the essence of the situation. The more stuff there is out there, the longer the neck becomes.

How does that happen? Well, when analyzing 1,000 search terms, for example, the top 50 search terms (5%) accounted for 31% of search volume. In other words, a small set of search terms were getting searched for again and again. However, when analyzing 5,000 search terms from the same search environment, the top 250 search terms (5%) accounted for 39% of search volume, an 8% increase. The Long Neck had gotten longer.

The more choice there is out there, the longer the neck becomes.

I call this the Bob Dylan effect. You can increase the number of singer-songwriters as much as you like, but there is still only one Bob Dylan.

We are living through an Information Big Bang. How on earth is the most important stuff going to get found? When your customers have so much choice, why should they read or view your stuff? Furthermore, why should they act based on what they have read?

If you want to make an impact—and avoid ending up in the Dead Zone—you need to understand the Long Neck. If you want to influence the impatient stranger—that's to say, if you want people to buy, to follow a new policy, to decide in your favor, to think that what you say has value—you need to understand *their* Long Neck: the things that really matter to them.

Understanding what really matters to a stranger is the single biggest challenge in web management. I once worked with a car manufacturer whose product managers and engineers thought that words like "engine" and "brand" were really important to their customers. But the words that actually mattered to their customers were "affordability", "reliability", and "low fuel consumption".

So, an organization may be focused on the same basic things as its customers, but if it uses the wrong words to describe them, then it's speaking a different language. You'll find an "engine" in the Long Neck of an "engineer", but it's "reliability" that the customer really cares about.

Your Long Neck and a stranger's Long Neck are rarely the same. You must accept that and work with it. If you can manage your Web site from the stranger's point of view, then everyone can succeed. In our increasingly interconnected world—the essence of which is the Web—this is not a utopian dream but a utilitarian necessity.

THREE IDEAS

Sean Wilentz is the author of the book *The Age of Reagan*. Talking about Reagan to *Newsweek*, he stated: "The key is to understand the economy of leadership: You should have ideas but they should be clear, but most of all they should be few—three at the most. Rearm the country, cut the weight of government, and win the cold war. After that we'll see. That's what Napoleon said: 'You win and then we'll see'."

So, here are the three ideas of this book:

1. **Know the stranger's Long Neck.** It is far more important to understand the Long Neck than the Long Tail. You might think that the Long Neck is obvious. Not so, and often what *you* think the Long Neck is, may not be what *your customers* think it is.

2. **Continuously improve your top tasks.** The Long Neck is made up of a small set of top tasks and it's important to manage them through a process of continuous improvement. To manage, you need to measure, and what you measure is your customers' ability to complete these tasks. The three key measures are: Task success rate, disaster rate, and completion time. (A disaster is where a customer thinks they've got the right answer but it's wrong.)

3. **Manage with facts, not opinion.** A key shift in the modern world is a shift away from opinion and gut instinct, to hard data. Evidence is customer centric. Opinion is organization centric.

chapter 2

Gut instinct and the information tsunami

Most results in probability are entirely counterintuitive.

Nassim Nicholas Taleb

One thing we've seen over and over is that decision makers overestimate the power of their own intuitions.

Ian Ayres

DID HE REALLY WIN?

"Seeing wasn't believing," stated an August 16, 2008 Associated Press story. "It took technology to confirm Michael Phelps won his seventh Olympic gold medal in the 100-meter butterfly with a finish so close it fooled the human eye."

But then it's fairly easy to fool the human eye. After all, most of us think we see depth when we look at the flat canvas of a picture. Phelps had beaten Milorad Cavic of Serbia and the Serbians accepted the ruling because "It was not the human eye making the judgement," said referee Ben Ekumbo of Kenya, a member of FINA's technical committee. "It was the footage."

"The video says [Phelps] finished first," said Branislav Jevtic, Serbia's chief of mission in Beijing. "In my opinion, it's not right, but we must follow the rules. Everybody saw what happened."

It's not right, but we must follow the rules. Everybody saw what happened so we know who really won. I've thought this way a million times myself. As an avid sports fan—a recovering fanatic of sorts—I have looked at referees with evil intent whenever they've made blatantly wrong decisions. It is, of course, scientifically proven that awful refereeing decisions only affect the team *you* support.

This book is about evidence-based decision making—facts, not opinion.

THE WORST POSSIBLE WAY TO DESIGN A WEB SITE

The worst possible way to design a Web site is to have five smart people in a room drinking lattes and posting Post-it note ideas. The longer you leave them in the room, the worse the design will become. It's a proven fact.

The second-worst way is to have 10 customers in a room drinking lattes and giving their opinion on what they want from a Web site. Opinion is death. Opinion is the plague. When it comes to Web site management, trusting your gut is the last thing you should do.

This book is about evidence-based decision making—facts, not opinion. It is about a management model that uses evidence of what customers actually do on a Web site, not what they say they do. I will prove to you throughout this book that you can trust neither your opinion nor your customers' opinions. I will give you techniques that will deliver statistically defensible evidence on your customers' actual behavior on your Web site.

THE EYES DECEIVE

A big problem with food in 19th-century England was that many people were far more interested in how it looked than how it tasted. They wanted the whitest of white breads, the greenest of green vegetables, and sweets that would glow in the dark. The color of the food you ate was a fashion and social class statement. Copper, Cornish clay, red lead, and all sorts of other adulterations, were used to make foods look good at the cost of the health—and sometimes the lives—of the people who ate them. The eyes deceived.

"There are two sides to the design coin. There is serious design—making sure that the manufactured object performs its task in the best possible way. And there is styling—the essentially superficial task of making sure something looks attractive," stated product designer James Dyson during his 2009 Richard Dimbleby Lecture.

Dyson went on to say that, "Styling for its own sake is a lazy 20th-century conceit, one that has passed its sell-by date." Would that it were so. But stylists know something very important about human nature: We buy, eat, and drink with our eyes. And it is easy to deceive the eyes, to make something look like more than it actually is. In many ways it's the essence of advertising and marketing—perception is everything.

Many Web sites suffer from SMOS (Senior Manager Opinion Syndrome). Senior managers, who don't give enough genuine attention to their Web sites, do manage to find the time to throw off casual opinions like: "The Web site needs to be more interactive, dynamic." Because these senior managers don't genuinely engage with web strategy, they become focused on superficial things like the visual design.

I have seen a boardroom of directors argue for ages about the colors on the homepage. The content on the Web site was awful, the navigation structure was appalling, the search engine couldn't have been any worse, and yet all that these very important people cared about was the colors on the homepage and having a design that was dynamic and interactive. We need to change that way of thinking and one of the very best ways to do so is by Web site management based on clear, defensible evidence.

The financial crisis that started in 2008 showed that more information does not lead to better decision making.

INFORMATION TSUNAMI AND YOU

Most business information is unmanaged. If you're involved in a Web site, you're involved in the management of information (content) and that is going to be one of the most crucial skills of the 21st century.

We need new tools, new techniques, new management approaches. Because trusting your gut instinct to find your way through 300 million exabytes is like asking a goldfish to memorize all the content on Wikipedia. Right now, most organizations simply don't have the skills or processes to manage such vast quantities of content.

You can help develop these skills by focusing on managing the tasks that the content must support. Don't make the common mistake of managing the technology or the content itself. Manage the tasks your customers need to complete, using the content that your organization publishes. This book will show you how.

TOO MUCH FINANCIAL INFORMATION

There has never been more information in the world, yet the financial crisis that started in 2008 showed that more information does not lead to better decision making. In the financial crisis of 1907 at least the bankers knew what they owed, what was owed to them, and what they owned.

Robert Bruner and Sean Carr, authors of *The Panic of 1907*, wrote that: "J. P. Morgan and his men had direct access to the books of nearly every troubled institution, enabling them to fairly appraise their value." However, in our current age, "despite mandated regulatory reporting, it is difficult, if not impossible, for financial decision-makers to know with clarity what is going on."

This tsunami of information is increasing in complexity, thus making it harder to make good decisions. Your job is to give your customers quick and easy access to the right information so that they can make good decisions.

"The ability to create, accumulate and distribute information is incalculably greater today than ever before and the pace of each of these activities is breakneck and increasing," wrote Stephen Spinelli Jr., President of Philadelphia University, in 2009. "No one knows how to effectively manage and discern the value and complexity of this information."

It is wrong to assume that digital natives will cope with ease no matter how much information is thrown at them.

INFORMATION OVERLOAD: A GENERATIONAL THING?

There is an argument that information overload is only an issue for older people (those over 30). "The BlackBerry® is a source of information overload to people who experience information overload—mostly those over age 30," according to a *Business Week* article. "To those under age 30, they are so good at managing the fast and endless flow of huge amounts of information, that they do not experience a feeling of information overload. They are in permanent sift-and-synthesize mode."

So, we just have to wait until everyone over 30 retires and the problem of information overload will be no more? Maybe it's not quite so simple. A 2008 Associated Press study on how young people consume news found that participants "showed signs of news fatigue; that is, they appeared debilitated by information overload and unsatisfying news experiences. Many consumers in the study were so overwhelmed and inundated by news that they just did not know what to do."

It is to be expected that young people will adapt better than older people to this explosion of information because they are "digital natives". But it is wrong to assume that digital natives will cope with ease no matter how much information is thrown at them.

TECHNOLOGY IS NOT MAGIC

The technology romantics have a wonderful belief in technology. Chris Anderson, editor of *Wired* and author of the bestselling book *The Long Tail*, is a huge believer in "filters". He correctly points out that the Long Tail can be full of crap but expects that with the right technology [filter] everyone will be able to sift through the tail and find exactly what they need.

In my experience of working with hundreds of organizations over the last 15 years, we have a long, long way to go before these filters will work well. And without changes in how we create and manage information they will never be truly effective. Most organizations do not even have the most basic capacities to manage information in a way that it is filterable. It's the classic "garbage in, garbage out" problem. This is the challenge. This is the opportunity.

chapter 3

From Long Tail to Dead Zone

The plural of anecdote is not data.
Ben Goldacre

Simplicity is not natural. You have to choose to make it happen.
Edward de Bono

FAMINE IN THE LONG TAIL

The Long Tail can be a place of obscurity and complexity. If it is not properly managed, it will destroy value rather than create it.

In 2007, of the nearly four million songs available on iTunes, 24% sold only one copy each and 91% sold less than 100 copies. "The Internet offers us a buffet of everything – and yet we're mainly settling for the likes of *The Love Guru* and *You Don't Mess With the Zohan*," wrote Farhad Manjoo, author of the book *True Enough*.

A study by *Billboard* found that hit songs accounted for more of the marketplace in 2009 than they did in 2004, with the top 200 songs making up more than one sixth of online music sales in 2009.

"Ever-increasing choice was supposed to mean the end of the blockbuster," *The Economist* stated in 2009. "It has had the opposite effect...In Britain, sales of the 10 bestselling books increased from 3.4m to 6m between 1998 and 2008...Between 2004 and 2008 films costing more than $100m to produce consistently returned greater profits to the big studios than cheaper films did."

In a world that is increasingly running on content, the quality of content—rather than the quantity of content—determines success.

"In a globally integrated market, blockbuster brands that address common consumer needs are more important than ever," according to Harvard Business School marketing professor, John Quelch.

The Long Tail—the term originally coined by Chris Anderson—describes "the niche strategy of businesses such as Amazon.com or Netflix that sell a large number of unique items, each in relatively small quantities," according to Wikipedia. The Long Tail concept states that with endless and easy choice, we will do endless choosing and buying of esoteric stuff.

Should your intranet publish every piece of Long Tail content the organization creates? Should a government Web site publish every piece of available content because the more information you make freely available, the better off society will be? Is the business model of the future about focusing on creating more and more products and services, thus making you money by selling less of more? Can you really make a profit that way?

The evidence so far is not convincing. However, perhaps it is too early to judge Long Tail economics. This may indeed be a business model of the future, though it may take another 10 years before it delivers value for most organizations.

What is beyond doubt is that the blockbuster is alive and well and delivering healthy profits. The top tasks in the Long Neck are super-critical to get right. By far the most value is in the Long Neck. Apple discovered that. Pixar discovered that. In a world that is increasingly running on content, the quality of content—rather than the quantity of content—determines success.

"It was a compelling idea," wrote Anita Elberse, associate professor of business administration in the marketing unit at Harvard Business School in 2008. "In the digitized world, there's more money to be made in niche offerings than in blockbusters. The data tells a different story."

There is no question that the tail exists and that it is getting longer. In an analysis of 5,500 titles by Nielsen VideoScan from January 2000 to August 2005, Elberse found that sales shifted "measurably into the tail: The number of titles that sold only a few copies almost doubled for any given week from 2000 to 2005. In the same period, however, the number of titles with no sales at all in a given week quadrupled."

This is important. It seems that at a certain point in the tail we reach the badlands, a dead zone, where stuff may live but where making a living is impossible.

The Nielsen VideoScan research also showed that "success is concentrated in ever fewer best-selling titles at the head of the distribution curve. From 2000 to 2005 the number of titles in the top 10% of weekly sales dropped by more than 50%—an increase in concentration that is common in winner-takes-all markets. The importance of individual best sellers is not diminishing over time. It is growing."

So, the Long Tail may be getting longer, but so too is the Long Neck.

You would think that if less money is being spent on the goods of megastars, then independent artists would be getting more money and thus making a better living. Not true, according to Elberse. "A more significant trend is that independent artists have actually lost their share among the more popular titles to superstar artists on the major labels," she writes. "The data shows how difficult it is to profit from the tail."

While the tail is very interesting the vast majority of revenue remains in the head.

THE REAL VALUE IS IN THE LONG NECK

Of the 13 million digital music tracks available in 2007, 10 million didn't sell a single copy. This is according to a study by Will Page, chief economist of the MCPS-PRS Alliance, the not-for-profit royalty collection society.

Here are some of the key findings of the study:

- 80% of the tracks monitored sold nothing at all in 2007
- Approximately 80% of sales revenue came from around 3% of the active tracks
- Only 40 tracks sold more than 100,000 copies, accounting for 8% of the business
- 80% of all revenue came from around 52,000 tracks

"My argument, in summary, was that the future of business is definitely not selling 'less of more'," Page told Telco 2 in 2008.

"Scale matters. Is the 'future of business' really selling less of more? Absolutely not. If Top of the Pops still existed, it would feature the Top 14, not Top 40."

Google is sometimes given as an example of the Long Tail at work. "I would like to tell you that the Internet has created such a level playing field that the Long Tail is absolutely the place to be—that there's so much differentiation, there's so much diversity, so many new voices," Google C.E.O Eric Schmidt told *McKinsey Quarterly* in 2008. "Unfortunately, that's not the case…So, while the tail is very interesting the vast majority of revenue remains in the head. And this is a lesson that businesses have to learn. While you can have a Long Tail strategy, you better have a head, because that's where all the revenue is."

This book is about giving you a head (Long Neck) strategy. About helping you use clear evidence to identify the top tasks in your Long Neck. In music and books it's easy to identify the U2s and Harry Potters of the Long Neck, but in other areas the Long Neck can be surprisingly difficult to identify. But there are always top tasks, whether you are managing an intranet, a government, university, or business Web site.

Eric Schmidt thinks that it's even more important to understand the blockbuster (top task) today because we may be on the verge of the global blockbuster. "It's probable that the Internet will lead to larger blockbusters and more concentration of brands," he told *McKinsey*. "Which, again, doesn't make sense to most people, because it's a larger distribution medium. But when you get everybody together they still like to have one superstar. It's no longer a US superstar, it's a global superstar."

We're all individuals, right? And the young digital native generation—with so much information and choice literally at their thumb-tips—will be the most liberated and individual of all. 'Far from liberating us, the proliferation of choice that modern technology has brought is overwhelming us—making us even more reliant on outside cues to determine what we like," writes

New Scientist. So what's the bottom line here? In an age of information overload it has never been more important to properly manage Long Neck tasks.

IN DEFENSE OF THE TAIL

Chris Anderson never said that the blockbuster would disappear. What he said was that it would decline in influence. He still has a good case. He points out that percentages can be misleading. He states that in Anita Elberse's analysis of the Rhapsody data, she finds that the top 10% of titles account for 78% of sales and that the top 1% account for 32%. "That sounds pretty concentrated around the head, until you reflect, as she notes, that '1% of a million is still 10,000...equal to the entire music inventory of a typical Wal-Mart store'," writes Anderson.

Most tails are getting longer and most necks are getting thinner. As Google's Eric Schmidt puts it, "We love the Long Tail, but we make most of our revenue in the head, because of the math of the power law. And you need both, by the way. You need the head and the tail to make the model work."

There is nothing wrong in having a Long Tail strategy but it is far more important to have a Long Neck strategy. If you have limited management resources, focus them on Long Neck tasks. And also remember that by introducing Long Tail tasks on to your Web site you may make it harder for your customers to find and complete Long Neck tasks.

chapter 4

The rise of the Long Neck

The lesson is simple:
Complexity kills.

Michael Dell

FOCUSING ON TOP TASKS

If there are four tasks/options/features that influence a choice, then chances are that one or two of these are top tasks. Let's say you wanted to buy a mobile phone and Manufacturer A has made an incredibly simple phone with four features, each of which facilitates a task. In deciding to buy this mobile phone you're going to have two top tasks:

- making calls
- taking calls

In this very simplified environment your top tasks represent 50% of the feature set. Now, let's say you are also shown a mobile phone from Manufacturer B. This phone has 100 features. Your top tasks will still be making and taking calls. There might be perhaps three more. Based on the analysis of some 60,000 people choosing their top tasks, we have found that if there are 100 tasks to choose from there will be five top tasks and about 10 fairly important ones. But we have never found a situation where in a range of 100 tasks, 50 are top tasks.

What does this mean? In the product—in this case, the mobile phone—that you need, there are usually really important reasons (top tasks) why you need it. In most situations these top tasks are relatively finite. So, the task range (feature set) might explode but the top tasks remain relatively fixed.

What are the implications? When things get incredibly complex we can be in danger of being caught up and carried away by the complexity, forgetting the top tasks we need the product for in the first place, or finding it difficult to quickly and clearly identify these top tasks. We are initially so impressed that the mobile phone can take pictures and play music that we might forget to check how easy it is to make and receive calls.

In 2004, there were 255 links on the Yahoo homepage.

MANAGING COMPLEXITY

Managing a large Web site involves managing complexity. Most intranets are good examples of what happens when you don't manage complexity, with their poorly organized architecture and out-of-date, low-quality content.

"Look at what Steve Jobs did when he took over Apple," wrote legendary marketer Al Ries for *Advertising Age* in 2008. "At the time, Apple marketed some 40 different products, from inkjet printers to the Newton handheld. On the computer side of Apple's business, there were four major lines (Quadras, Power Macs, Performas, and PowerBooks) each with a dozen different models, a typical megabrand product lineup. Jobs cut the product line down to four machines: Two laptops and two desktops. He later told *BusinessWeek*, 'Everything just got simpler. That's been one of my mantras—focus and simplicity.'"

When General Motors announced its restructuring, it did not talk about expanding the range of products it would deliver to customers. Rather, it was about focus, about reducing the number of brands.

The comparison between Google and Yahoo is instructive. Google has had a relentless focus on making the top task of search easy to do. Yahoo has tried to be everything to everybody, and has more often put the advertiser, rather than the customer, first.

In 2004, there were 255 links on the Yahoo homepage. "After looking over the history of Yahoo's homepages since 1994, it has pretty much told a story of a site with increasingly smaller font size and more stuff packed on it," Kara Swisher wrote for the *Wall Street Journal* in July 2009. According to Tapan Bhat, senior vice president of Integrated Consumer Experiences at Yahoo, "It had nothing to do with the user, but what Yahoo wanted the user to do." The year 2004 was a nadir for Yahoo complexity, with 255 links on its homepage. By 2006 it had 168 links on its homepage. By 2007 it had 139. By 2008 it had 119 and by 2009 it had about 100.

Every time you add, you add complexity.

TINY TASKS HURT TOP TASKS

Choice is good. "Today the grocery store carries more than 20 different types of flour, ranging from such basics as whole wheat and organic varieties to exotics such as amaranth and blue cornmeal. There is, amazingly enough, already a Long Tail in flour," writes Chris Anderson.

Too much choice is not so good. What is commonly not understood is that when choice is increased it can often have a negative impact on the most popular choices (top tasks). Sometimes you just want the most popular version of a particular product. You go to the store and you can find all sorts of esoteric versions but not the most popular one.

"Last week I went to my local supermarket for Pillsbury's Best all-purpose flour, a brand I have been buying for years," wrote Al Ries for *Advertising Age* in 2008. "No luck. The store had Pillsbury's Best bread flour, whole wheat flour, self-rising flour, and unbleached all-purpose flour. They just didn't have the original Pillsbury's Best all-purpose flour. So I bought Gold Medal all-purpose flour instead."

This is one of the most important points of this book. Every time you add, you add complexity. The tiny tasks nibble away at the top tasks. There are so many of them that, little by little, they build up a critical mass and eventually smother the top tasks.

Move away from the launch-and-leave culture towards continuous improvement and testing of top tasks.

OBSERVE AND ADAPT

In an increasingly complex world it is becoming more and more difficult to predict and plan ahead. So what do you do? Well, the Web has at least part of the answer. You become flexible, responsive and adaptable. You need a strategy and a vision for sure. However, you have to be able to constantly tweak it based on feedback from your environment.

In his excellent book, *The Black Swan*, Nassim Nicholas Taleb provides ample evidence that in highly complex environments prediction and expert opinion is a dangerous game. He writes about how people are particularly poor at understanding the impact of top tasks such as blockbusters. He stresses how more information, particularly if it is Long Tail information, can lead to poorer decisions. "Additional knowledge of the minutiae of daily business can be useless, even actually toxic," he writes. The bottom line for Taleb is "Be prepared!"

There is a range of studies and concepts such as the butterfly effect that indicate that in highly complex environments we must develop a rapid testing-and-adaptation approach rather than a planning-and-prediction approach. So how do we do this?

On one level, the Web is a very cold and unresponsive environment. However, there are methods of working with the Web that will enable you to get amazing feedback from your customers on an ongoing basis, and this book is about giving you some of these methods. Google rarely launches fully fledged spanking new products. Instead, it launches betas—software which has been through initial testing and is then released to the general public for further testing—that it then rapidly and continuously improves based on feedback. This is the way to go.

Which leads to another key idea of this book: The need to move away from the launch-and-leave culture towards continuous improvement and testing of top tasks based on the observed behavior of your customers. It's a shift away from products to services, from production to service. In a world where it's becoming more and more difficult to predict what customers will want, it's essential to launch and test. If predicting is difficult, test and improve instead. Get the site up and evolve it based on a continuous feedback loop: The eternal beta.

Of course, continuous improvement is only possible if you have a relatively small number of tasks to manage. If you have a massive Long Tail of stuff that you're pulling behind you, then there is little hope of continuous improvement.

chapter 5

A secret method for understanding your customers

Most things survive because they are adequate; because they are not problems; and because no one has set out to challenge them. They may be far from the simplest way of doing things.

Edward de Bono

LISTEN CAREFULLY

What I'm about to tell you is a secret. It is a method that will give you tremendous insight into what your customer's Long Neck is. And why is it a secret? Not because it's hidden, not because it's unknown. No, it's a secret because the accepted wisdom is that this method cannot work, it doesn't make sense. Over the years whenever an expert in market or consumer research looks at this method they withdraw in shock. They are aghast, stunned that anyone in their right mind could, for a single moment, think that it is a good method for understanding human behavior.

"It simply can't work," one such market research expert said to me. "You can't give people a list of 100 tasks and ask them to choose the five most important."

"It does work," I replied. "I understand why you think it can't work, but it does. It has worked for Microsoft, Schlumberger, Cisco, and Tetra Pak, to name just a few."

"It can't work. It goes against 50 years of theory. Everyone knows that you can't give people more than 10 options, 20 maximum."

"That's what I thought too," I replied. "But I have tested this over the years. I have the results of over 60,000 voters in many different organizations in many different countries and in many different languages, and it does absolutely work. Crystal clear trends emerge. It helps you to identify the top tasks—Long Neck—of your customers. It works."

"It can't work. I don't believe you."

And so the conversations have gone on with research experts. It is always the experts, by the way, who are so trenchant, so unyielding. I offer to show them the data, but so far none of them has accepted. They simply don't care about the data, the evidence. It has to be wrong, because it goes against accepted theory, common sense, how they've been trained. Without any analysis or further investigation, it has to be wrong. People will choose randomly when given a hundred tasks or other such options, these experts say. But it does work. And so it's our secret—just between you and me. That is, of course, if I can convince you that it works. I'm going to share the history of this approach with you, how it evolved. I'm going to give you lots and lots of data, lots of case studies from real companies who have used it to improve their public Web sites and intranets.

COULDN'T AFFORD THE T-SHIRT

I grew up on a small farm in rural Ireland. We didn't even have a tractor, let alone a computer. We were poor and miserable. But then, the Irish have made an industry out of being poor and miserable. Only an Irishman (Samuel Beckett) could say: "I can't go on, I won't go on, I'll go on."

Anyway, when I was young I used to love watching Westerns and those wagons going out West. I felt like I'd never get a chance to be part of something like that—the opening up of a new world. But I promised myself that if I ever did see those wagons going out West again, I'd have to get on one. And the first time I saw the Web in 1993, I saw those wagons…

I've been involved in managing and consulting on Web sites since 1994 and was part of the whole dot com mania. Companies I founded received millions in investments, and I became arrogant and conceited (I still am, I suppose). I made more mistakes in a couple of years than most people make in a lifetime. In 2000 I owned a company valued at $200 million. In 2001 it went bust, I'd been there, done that and I couldn't even afford the T-shirt. It's not easy to stand up in front of over 100 people and tell them they have lost their jobs, especially after having made all sorts of (perhaps deluded) promises. It's a very humbling experience.

In 2001, as I sifted through the ruins, I pulled out the core ideas that had helped us become successful in the first place. They were covered in ashes and burnt at the edges, but once I rubbed them with my sleeve they still shone a little. These core ideas were:

- This is the age of the customer; the Web signals a shift in power away from experts and organizations to individuals and the groups they form
- As the quantity of content explodes the stuff that really matters to people remains fairly constant—the Long Neck is getting longer
- Web management must not be about opinion or gut instinct; it must be about evidence, data
- While traditional marketing is about getting attention, web marketing and communication must be about giving attention—there is a world of difference between the two

So, I got up again and got on the road and I've pretty much been on the road ever since. Half of my year is spent outside my home in Ireland. I've given talks and workshops in 35 countries. I've been to at least half the states in the United States. Very slowly I've built up a partnership again and we have had the privilege of working with many great organizations. And I've stayed relentlessly focused on this very core concept and idea.

Identify and continuously improve your customers' top tasks. Remember that tiny tasks can often hurt the performance of top tasks. You are not the customer. The customer is a stranger. Their top tasks are rarely the same as yours.

FROM CARD SORTING TO TASK VOTING

I started doing workshops on how to structure a Web site; how to organize the content and the navigation. I had been following many of the ideas of Jakob Nielsen—certainly the person who has most influenced my thinking on web management. (Jared Spool is another thinker I admire.) Around 2002, I read an article by James Robertson, a real pioneer of web management from Australia. He was talking about an idea called card sorting and how it could be used to help design a classification for a Web site. It was an inspiring piece and I decided to try the concept out.

The idea that everybody is different has probably contributed more than any other single factor to bad web design.

I chose the area of tourism because I thought it was something that everyone could relate to. I went out and analyzed lots of tourism and travel sites and, among other things, took down their first and second level classifications. Then I adapted the list into an Irish context, because I thought it would be easier to choose a particular country's Web site than to have a general tourism Web site.

In total, I gathered 146 tourism-related tasks or factors that influence the decision to choose a country as a destination for a vacation. Here's a sample of them:

About Ireland	Accommodation
Best of Ireland	Dublin
Irish Vacation Packages	Midlands East
Planning a Trip	Sights & Activities
Special Offers	What to See & Do

I carried a box of 20 sets of cards around with me, each set with 146 cards roughly the size of a business card and with one of the 146 phrases on each of them. At a certain point in the workshop I would hand the sets out to a group of two to four attendees and ask them to sort the cards into logical groups of classifications. It was an interesting exercise, but also quite time-consuming, and it was hard to discern if there were core trends and repeatable patterns emerging.

One of the things I was trying to do was to move web design and management beyond the whole craft focus that it was—and to a degree still is—embedded in. The crafts people believe that web design is an art that requires highly skilled people to implement, that it's a creative process and there are few repeatable rules, because it all depends on the Web site in question and the type of audience that comes to it. "Every Web site is different and every customer is different" might be the way to sum up this craft-focused belief.

If you agree with the above paragraph, you should probably stop reading now because the rest of this book is really going to irritate you. It's not that I want you to stop—I'm honored that you are investing your time in reading this—but I don't want to waste your time by putting forward a range of arguments that you might strongly disagree with and have absolutely no interest in implementing.

Still here? Good. The idea that everybody is different has probably contributed more than any other single factor to bad web design and management. It resulted in great big, bumbling, chaotic, and unmanaged Web sites. It has led to hugely expensive, wasteful, and often utterly useless portal implementations where information technology resources were focused on cool and fancy concepts such as personalization, when they should have been focusing on ensuring that the Web site was kept up to date with quality content. (What do you get when you personalize crap content? Personalized crap.)

This book is about management metrics that make sense, about evidence you can bring to senior management and defend.

THE PURSUIT OF REPEATABLE TRENDS

Frederick Taylor is regarded by many as the father of management. He once quoted his own father as saying to him: "Any time you start poking under the cover of something or looking into something you begin to find laws. These are the laws of creation, or of nature, or something. They're there." Management is about identifying these laws, these repeatable trends.

So, I was looking for repeatable trends, and the basic card-sorting approach, while definitely useful, was not quite what I needed. I started experimenting. Instead of getting people to sort all the cards into bunches, I started asking them to pick out the cards they thought contained the most important words that should appear on the homepage of this imaginary Irish tourism Web site.

Some trends began to emerge. Then I started limiting the number of cards they could choose to 10. Stronger trends emerged. Then I started giving people less time to choose. Stronger trends emerged. Then I started getting people to vote. They had to choose the most important one, the next most important one, and so on. Even stronger, clearer trends became obvious. People started choosing the same cards for their top 10 and, when they had to vote, certain choices really began to rise to the top. And the funny thing was that the less time I gave people, the more consistent the voting patterns became.

Again and again, people told me that they couldn't possibly choose 10 out of 146, and certainly not in the time that I was giving them. And then I had a great idea. I started the sorting just before lunch. I told participants that the quicker they finished, the quicker they could go to lunch.

The cards were spread out all over tables and floors. It was like a massive jigsaw set. I asked them to stop thinking too much and just choose what jumped out at them. Not to examine each and every card in great detail, but to simply hunt out the cards that contained the words that meant most to them.

It was amazing. After going through this process with over 1,000 people in 11 different countries, there was an extraordinary consistency of choice. Two tasks—"accommodation" and "special offers"—got 18% of the vote. Whether in New Zealand, Australia, the United Kingdom or the United States, it really didn't matter—people were making the same choices again and again. And when I compared these choices to what the leading Web sites in the travel industry were doing, they mapped very well. On the homepages of these Web sites were booking processes for accommodation along with deals and special offers.

In order to allow people to record their votes for their top 10 choices I created a simple one-page printout with all the phrases listed in three columns in alphabetical order. After having chosen their 10 cards, I would ask people to place a 10 beside their most important choice, a nine beside their next most important choice, and so on. Then something a bit strange began to happen. Certain participants started cheating.

LUNCH-SEEKING CHEATERS

Instead of going through all the hassle of spreading the cards out and diligently sorting through them, these lunch-seeking cheating attendees went straight to the alphabetical list and started putting their scores in directly. I was annoyed. I told them that they needed to go through the card-sorting process because there was something special in this process that would get much better results than if they simply voted using the A–Z list.

There was another reason. I had invested a lot of time and energy in card sorting. I would enthusiastically explain it and espouse it. And I had spent ages and ages in the mind-numbing activity of printing out all of the cards and sorting them into bundles, and buying a big batch of elastic bands to keep them together. (Those bloody elastic bands kept snapping.) And after searching and searching, I finally found the perfect way to transport them; a plastic toolbox. I did look like a bit of a fool walking through airports with a plastic toolbox, but I swear there's no better way to store 20 sets of 146 cards. And sometimes the card sets would get mixed up, so I put a unique letter of the alphabet on the back of each...I'll stop now. (I could go on.) I was very proud of my cards and I didn't want to see all my effort and energy wasted.

And then someone challenged me: "Why do I have to sort these cards? Why can't I just vote based on this list?"

"Well, you can't," I said to him. "You can't, because card-sorting is a proven method that works. There's something about sorting the cards that helps you clarify what is really important to you. Just choosing from a list will never work as well."

Over time, more and more people tried to cheat. I sat in my hotel room one night thinking about how cruel people are. And then I began thinking about the whole process of card sorting. (That's pretty sad, isn't it?) Why is card sorting better than voting on the list, I wondered? It takes longer, it's more hands-on and interactive, so it must be better. And, of course, it has a proven history and I had spent so much time preparing all those cards. That was a lot of hard work. And I had gotten up in front of a lot of audiences and passionately explained how it was such a good process, how it was better than the others. I was the teacher and it couldn't be that my students had discovered a better method all by themselves.

But I really didn't have a precise answer as to why it was better than simply voting on a list. So, reluctantly, I decided to test it. I was sure it wouldn't work, but it was worth a try. One brave cold morning I hugged my red toolbox, left it in the hotel room, and walked with great trepidation towards the workshop. I just gave people A4 pages with three columns of tiny text listing 146 tourism tasks. I asked people to quickly choose their top 10 by scanning the list.

To my great surprise, when I added up the results, I found that the voting patterns were almost identical to the ones from workshops where I had used the card sorting approach. I tested again. I found similar patterns. The same top tasks kept coming out in front:

- **Accommodation**
- **Special offers**

This shouldn't have happened. You can't give people 146 choices and find consistency. Not just consistency. "Accommodation" and "Special Offers" got 18% of the vote between them. That's extraordinary consistency. Out of 146 choices, two get 18% of the vote. Something very interesting was happening. In Australia, New Zealand, Ireland, Britain and the United States, the same choices were being made.

We often have too much invested in our theories. We become emotional about them.

WHY THIS METHOD WORKS

I sat around with tourism experts and asked them what people really wanted from a tourism Web site. I observed conversations that became more and more convoluted, more and more about branding and experience and philosophy. And the more these experts talked, the more they seemed to miss the point. They couldn't grasp the essence of what a country destination Web site should be: Accommodation and special offers. People needed a place to sleep and they wanted a good deal, a special offer. It just reinforced what I had found out through many years of bitter experience:

The worst possible way to design a Web site is to have five smart people in a room drinking lattes discussing branding.

Some ideas emerged:

1. The Web is about basic human drives and emotions. A great way to understand these needs is to almost overload people with a very long list and get them to vote on the top five most important things to them. What's important to them jumps out from the subconscious.

2. It is essential that you limit the number of choices. We tested situations where people could choose as many as they liked from the list and the results were not useful at all. Some people selected whatever took their fancy; stuff that didn't really matter to them but that they thought might matter to them. And because they could choose whatever they wanted they chose a huge range of stuff.

3. It's important to limit it to five choices or fewer. We tested with 10 choices and found that a significant number of people struggled to select 10 things that really mattered to them. We found that after five choices, people began selecting things that might be of interest, but they didn't feel very strongly about. We need to get the stuff people feel strongly about.

4. It's essential that people vote. Voting does something to people. If they just have to select five tasks, that's one thing, but if they have to select the most important task to them and vote for it as the most important, that brings their choice to a new level of seriousness. We give people 15 votes and they have to give five to the most important, four to the next most important, and so on.

5. The less time you give people to vote, the more accurate the choices become. The less they "think", the better. If they scan the list, what really matters to them will jump out, and what doesn't matter will fade into the background. In a list of 100 I'd recommend that no more than five minutes is given to voting.

Giving people a list of 100 tasks and asking them to choose the five most important to them sounds mad. So why does it work? My colleague Gord Hopkins suggests one reason: The cocktail party effect. You're at a party. There are a lot of people in the room, a lot of buzz and noise. Across the crowded room someone mentions your name in conversation and out of the noise there's clarity; you hear your name being spoken. The words jump out at you.

What I have noticed is that people don't read the whole list. They just scan it, and out jump the things that really matter to them. It's not that they discover things on the list that interest them. It's that inside their brains there are things that really matter to them. And seeing these things on the list is a reinforcement of something that they already care about a lot.

A key factor in getting it all to work involves making sure that you choose the words in the list very carefully. They must be words that customers can understand and relate to. These words must reflect what the customer cares about, not what the organization cares about.

So, that's the secret about task identification. It wasn't really my idea at all. I didn't think it could work. To my "expert" sensibility it didn't make sense until I saw it for myself. It happened through a process of interacting with my audience and observing what they were doing. Which is exactly how you should manage your Web site—through observation and the willingness to apprentice yourself to your customers, to learn from their behavior, and make changes as required.

This task identification method doesn't make common sense but it does work. Go for the evidence, not the theory. Often, we have too much invested in our theories. We become emotional about them. We defend them not because they are the right things to defend, but because they are right for us. But what we really need to know is what is right for our customers.

Voting, it seems, makes people very focused.

A CONTRADICTION

So, you're probably thinking here: Hold on a minute. This guy is talking about simplicity and the need to make top tasks easier to find and complete, yet he says that people can choose logically from a list of 100 choices. Isn't that a contradiction? And I have to agree with you, there is a certain amount of contradiction in it.

Here's my rationale: This is a survey, a vote. Scanning the list is not the same as scanning a webpage where there are graphics, layout, and different types of content to deal with and where the links may be placed in several different positions on the page. I have found that people don't really scan a webpage in its entirety. Rather, they scan segments of the page, and will often entirely miss what they are looking for if it happens to not be in the segment they are scanning.

The person is scanning a single list, and this list has been very carefully selected so as to contain words that really matter to the person. Before I added the request to vote, the results of the approach were much less useful. Voting, it seems, makes people very focused.

chapter 6

There are always tasks

In physics, order is the same thing as information.

Eric D. Beinhocker

WE DON'T HAVE TASKS 'ROUND HERE

Some years ago I stood in front of an audience in Chicago extolling the virtues of task management. A hand was raised in the audience.

"I can see how managing tasks might work for some Web sites but it wouldn't work for ours," the lady said. "Because we don't have tasks. We have information."

"What sort of Web site do you have?" I asked.

"A health Web site."

"A health Web site? Okay. Let's say my child has a rash," I replied. "When I come to your Web site, am I looking for information or am I looking to get rid of the rash?"

Nobody cares about information for its own sake, except the creators of said information. The customer has a task they want to complete, a problem they want to solve. Information is only useful in the context of the task.

Information has become an awful, vulgar, terrible, atrocious word. Its usage should be banned within all decent, morally upright organizations. Information is the root of all evil when it comes to the professional management of Web sites. Information is why we get the long useless tail and dead zone of useless information. Information is why we get content that is unreadable, that is too long, too complicated, too propagandist. Information is why we have content written by people who can't even follow their own instructions.

Many organizations are producing information today as if they were producing works of modern art: It just exists for its own sake. It has no real function, no real role, and doesn't support the completion of a task. It's just there to be collected by information lovers.

I say all this as someone who used to love collecting information. I remember many years ago, when I first arrived in America, I came out of the baggage claim area in JFK airport and saw a big sign: INFORMATION. I was so happy. Being the avid information collector, I dutifully queued up.

"Hello," I said, "How's it going? What's the weather like over here?" (We Irish love to talk about the weather.) The information professional gave me a New York stare and said: "Next!"

It was so great to be in New York. So, I dutifully queued up again. But this time I would be ready. No wasting time on trivial, throwaway weather requests.

"Hello," I said in a firm and determined tone. "Can I have some information, please?" He looked at me quizzically.

"Do you need a taxi?" he said.

"No, my cousin is picking me up at four," I replied.

"Do you need to book a hotel?"

"No. Sure, I'm staying with my cousin. He has a nice place out in Queens."

Later that evening, I tried my best to explain to the NYPD (New York Police Department) that we Irish just loved collecting information for its own sake. For its inherent beauty, balance, and most importantly, for its transcendent inner thinginess. But I've since recovered. I don't look for random pieces of information anymore, I promise.

A person who produces content without understanding the tasks the content needs to support is a dangerous person indeed.

THERE ARE ALWAYS TASKS

There are always tasks. You just have to root them out. Information in and of itself has no purpose. Treat information as a verb, not a noun. It is a process that supports a task; it is about the transfer of knowledge that results in some action. If information does not move your customers to do something, then it has failed. Creating it has been a waste of time and money.

Your customer always has a reason to look for this information. You just haven't discovered it yet. Information must have a purpose. It must support the completion of a task and, if it doesn't, then you must remove it from your Web site, or, better still, never publish it in the first place.

Finding information is often just a part of a broader task. A rash on a hand can be dealt with if the person finds the right information. But the information only serves a task—like minimizing pain, reducing swelling, taking medication, or going to a clinic. Information needs to be organized by how people are thinking when they need it. Furthermore, the health professionals who provide that information don't just want informed people, they want healthier people, people who act on the information. That is how health professionals know they have done a good job. It is the same with other information on the Web. Your content authors cannot measure how well they are doing unless viewers of their information take action that can be measured.

Many people who create information on Web sites are much more inclined to think of information as a noun, a thing. They have to get this thing done, this thing produced, this thing published, this thing put up. The life of the traditional communicator, of the web content professional, is a life of projects and events; a life of producing things, stuff. That's how they're measured and how they're rewarded—on the production of things.

Information is useless as a noun. A person who produces content without understanding the tasks the content needs to support is a dangerous person indeed, someone who's not to be trusted, to be kept well away from. Cross to the other side of the street when you see them coming. Because there approaches a put-it-upper (derived from the Latin *put-it-uppo*), whose function in life is to put things up on Web sites. By Wednesday at 4 p.m., if you can, please. Thanks. You're a great put-it-upper, you know.

THERE ARE HEALTH TASKS

The National Health Service's Web site for England (NHS Choices) gets millions of visitors every month. It's an excellent, trusted, and well managed Web site. And this is an important, perhaps obvious point: Nobody sets out to create a customer-hostile Web site. Few people start a content project with the objective of making the language impossible to understand, or making the navigation confusing. Web teams don't set out to make life miserable for their customers. It just happens. The internal pressures and needs of the organization, the very act of doing your job on a day-to-day basis, make it easy to lose sight of the customer.

NHS Choices is determined to be a truly customer-centric Web site. And it is. However, like even the best Web sites, it can always do a better job. So it asked my company (Customer Carewords) to carry out a task identification project to get a clearer sense of its customers' top tasks.

It was a fascinating project and the result was that there was a very clear top task that ran across every single segment of the population. It didn't matter if you were in Yorkshire or London, rich or poor, doctor or patient, someone with a long-term illness or a short-term one, a patient or caregiver, you had the same top task when you came to the NHS Choices Web site. (More about that top task later.)

A goal may have made you begin to change how you live but when you come to a Web site you have a task.

FROM GOALS TO TASKS

Before we could get people to vote on the tasks, we had to define them. We had to word them in language that was clear and easy to understand. This in itself is a thought-provoking process. Moving away from tools and technologies, organization departments, unit names and brand names, organization language and buzzwords, inside-thinking—moving away from all this and getting to the customers' tasks is a truly useful exercise.

Forget about the voting process. The very fact of defining and coming to an internal agreement on potential customer tasks can open the eyes of an awful lot of people. "So we have tasks after all," I often hear people say as we go through this process.

A good way to start identifying tasks is by examining your organization's objectives, strategy, mission statement, and other information that articulates what the organization is about and wants to achieve. Why does the organization exist? What does it see as its purpose? Where does it want to go over the next five years?

Simple as these questions are, many organizations do not have ready answers. This was not the case for NHS Choices. It had a very strong customer-centric ethos, a service focus. Among other things, it had articulated a significant number of customer goals. It saw its customers as primarily the general public, but also wanted the Web site to help doctors, nurses and other health professionals. It tried to get into the shoes of an ordinary person, to see the world through their eyes. Here are some of the Web site goals that NHS Choices felt ordinary people had:

● **I'd like to be happier**
● **I'd like to improve my family's health**
● **I'd like to have more energy**
● **Help me look after myself the best I can**
● **Help me improve my chances**

Here are some of the goals of doctors, nurses and other health professionals:

● **Give me information I can trust and refer patients to for further reading**
● **Give me material that helps me explain and discuss things with patients**
● **Give me material that helps me persuade patients to take responsibility for their health**
● **Help me understand what patients think about our service**

NHS Choices had these and many more goals, and they were an excellent source for the customer task longlist. However, goals must be translated into tasks, because Web sites are about tasks. A goal may have made you begin to change how you live but when you come to a Web site you have a task; a task that when completed will help you further your goal. As a web professional, it's not enough to know that your customers have goals like "I'd like to be happier" or "Help me look after myself the best I can" or "Help me improve my chances". These are important goals but what can you do to the Web site on Monday morning in order to help people achieve them?

We need customer tasks. We need clarity. You must make things very concrete and clear on your Web site, because people search and navigate with concrete tasks in mind; tasks they want to complete. The more ambiguous you are about your customers' tasks, the more likely you are to put up lots of vague, meaningless, or misleading information.

chapter 7

Defining tasks at NHS Choices

When we think of something as having design, we think of it as having a purpose—it is fit for a task…designs exhibit purpose.

Eric D. Beinhocker

SOURCES FOR THE TASK LONGLIST

The first step in task management is to carry out a task situation analysis in order to understand the whole range of customer tasks that exist. I call this list of customer tasks the "longlist".

The following longlist sources are specifically for a public Web site, but the basic approach to building a longlist works just as well for an intranet. (However, you can't really look at "competitor" intranets, and using public web search statistics is not relevant from an intranet perspective.)

1. **Organization strategy:** Analyze corporate philosophy, vision, and strategy statements. What does the organization want to achieve over the next five years, and specifically what does it want to achieve on the Web? It is very important that you link your Web site strategy to the overall strategy of the organization. This seems obvious, but strangely many Web sites are disconnected from core organizational aims and objectives.

2. **Stakeholder interviews:** Talk to key people within the organization and find out what they think the purpose of the Web site is. What do they think the customer's top tasks are? What do they think the top tasks should be?

3. **Examine existing Web site:** A good way to start is to copy levels one and two of the Web site classification into the longlist. Another good source is the site index.

4. **Analyze top search terms:** Do this by
   a. Analyze data from the Web site search engine. Try to get the top 100 search terms over a 12-month period.
   b. Google Adwords: **https://adwords.google.com/ select/KeywordToolExternal**. Enter important words and phrases to see how people are searching for them.

For example, when we tested for "flu" we noticed that the following terms were particularly searched for: Flu symptoms, swine flu symptoms.

   c. Google Trends: **http://www.google.com/trends**. If you want to do deeper research and compare search word trends over several years, then Google Trends is the place to go.

5. **Most visited webpages:** What were the top 100 most visited pages on the Web site over the last year? (For a smaller Web site, the top 50 would be enough.)

6. **Competitor or peer Web sites:** A minimum of four to six should be analyzed for tasks, particularly at the homepage level.

7. **Relevant media:** Are there magazines, specialist industry Web sites, associations, etc.?

8. **Customer feedback:** What are the most common customer inquiries and complaints? Talk to support, help, and sales staff to get this sort of data.

9. **Customer research:** Are there surveys or other research that show what tasks customers come to the Web site to complete?

10. **Customer interviews:** For a large project, I recommend doing 10–20 customer interviews. These interviews don't usually uncover new tasks outside those already discovered as a result of analyzing the sources above. However, interviews are great for getting a feel for how the customer thinks. And they can show you how tasks are carried out, which is often faster and more concrete than a

mere description. Make these interviews very short (about 15 minutes), using the following format:

   a. Brief introduction

   b. What are your top three tasks in this area?

   c. Please visit the Web site and try to complete one of these tasks. (You can do these interviews remotely using screen-sharing software.)

It's not a good idea to have a task name that is very heavily associated with one particular demographic.

DUPLICATES AND CATEGORY-SPECIFIC TASKS

We collect tasks in a spreadsheet with the following headings:

- **Tasks:** This is where we place the task word/phrase.
- **Duplicates:** This column contains task phrases that are very similar to each other.
- **Class:** This is the broad classification that the task phrase fits into.
- **Source:** This is where we got the task phrase. For example, "Top 100 Search Results".
- **Internal Source:** This identifies the person who put the task on the list. (Sometimes a number of people will be involved in the research process.)

As we assemble a longlist we may enter words that are exact duplicates or near-duplicates. In the following NHS Choices longlist we see that "Women's health" was found on the BBC health Web site and on webmd.com.

Tasks	Duplicate	Class	Source	Internal Source
Where can I find a diabetes clinic?			user goals doc	
Which health screenings do you need?			health.yahoo.com	
Women	Women		familydoctor.org	
Women's health	Women		bbc health	
Women's health	Women		webmd.com	
Women's health Information	Women		healthsites.co.uk	
Work gyms and performance			NHS Choices	
Workplace health			NHS Choices	
Your guide to the science in the news			NHS Choices	

We would immediately delete one of the "Women's health" entries. Now, what we have left is:

- **Women**
- **Women's health**
- **Women's health information**

At this early stage in the process, we don't need to delete any of these, but at some stage we would probably have to choose one and delete the others.

A larger point here is whether we should have a task connected with "women" at all because women are a category or segment of the population. If we do, shouldn't we have "Men's health" and "Children's health", as well as "Old people's health"? Think ahead to how this word will be used in navigational links. Isn't "Women's health" very vague and catch-all? It's not really a task but a whole collection of tasks.

Here are some things to consider:

1. It's not a good idea to have a task name that is very heavily associated with one particular demographic. It will likely get a high vote from that demographic but may not get a high vote from other demographics.

2. To identify the top tasks of a particular demographic we add a question that allows users to categorize themselves. (For example: What is your gender?) That way you can segment the data later and see if the top tasks are very different for each category segment or if there is overlap.

3. It's not a good idea to have a word in the final list that contains many tasks, because if it gets a high vote, you can't be sure as to what exactly was voted for. Remember, task identification is about action; it's about helping you change your Web site so your customers can more easily complete their tasks. You want clear results from this list so you can act on them decisively.

It is easy to fall into the trap of the organizational unit and departmental view of the world.

Thus, where possible, we create neutral tasks that are not specific to an audience or demographic. (They need to work for women, men, etc.) Here are some examples:

- appointment reminders
- avoiding and preventing disease
- basic facts about conditions/diseases

● **best place to go for help (GP, emergency, clinic, walk-in centre, pharmacist)**

These tasks could be important to both men and women. We let the voters decide.

In researching a condition/disease what five factors are most important to you?				
Tasks	Duplicate	Class	Source	Internal Source
Book your GP appointment online	appointment	Find services/ experts	patients.co.uk	
Let me book an appointment	appointment	Find services/ experts	user goals doc	
Make an appointment	appointment	Find services/ experts	mayoclinic.com	
Remind me when it's time for my appointment	appointment	Living with	user goals doc	
Request an appointment	appointment	Find services/ experts	netwellness	

The list of tasks in the preceding table has been marked as a duplicate of "appointment". However, if you analyze them you'll see that there are two distinct tasks:

● **book an appointment online**
● **appointment reminders**

The following tasks are all essentially the same and need to be merged into one:

● **Let me book an appointment**

Make an appointment
Request an appointment

As you do your task longlisting you will begin to get a sense of how popular or important a particular task is. This is because you will keep coming across it. It will be:

in the top level of your Web site classification;
on competitor Web sites;
in the top search results;
in the most downloaded pages;
in the top help desk queries.

Focusing on tasks can be a tremendously clarifying and in some cases liberating experience. (Maybe liberating is taking it a little too far.) It is easy to fall into the trap of the organizational unit and departmental view of the world, to get carried away by the technology or the cool brand name that someone came up with for an application or initiative. We so easily drift into the internal world of the organization. It's comforting. You make friends internally by focusing on things, on units of work, and on the elite language used by those in the know. It's hard to focus on the tasks of strangers.

It's essential to focus on customer tasks. This is the age of the customer, not the organization. The customer is on your Web site because they have a task to complete. Helping your organization to think about tasks is like cleaning a window in a derelict house— so much organizational dust has fallen. When you apply some good old elbow grease and wipe away the grime of internal thinking you see a new world outside.

One of the most important things the classifications help you do is divide the list into smaller chunks.

APPLYING TASK CLASSIFICATIONS

Classifying tasks is a way of grouping them to make it easier to get to the final shortlist. Classifications do not need to be exactly right because your customers will not see this list of classifications when they vote; they will only see a randomly ordered shortlist of tasks.

Below is a sample of the classifications used for NHS Choices.

1. Alternative

2. Causes/risk factors

3. Find services/experts

4. Live well/healthy living

5. News

6. Symptoms

7. Tests/diagnosis

8. Treatment

You can see how they were applied in the following table:

Tasks	Duplicate	Class	Source
Appointment reminders		Treatment	
Avoiding and preventing disease		Live well/ healthy living	Net doctor uk
Basic facts about conditions/ diseases		Tests/ diagnosis	NHSC
Best place to go for help (GP, A&E, clinic, walk-in centre, pharmacist)		Find services/ experts	
Body Mass Index (BMI) calculator		Live well/ healthy living	healthline.com
Book an appointment online		Treatment	
Can I get this on the NHS?		Treatment	
Can I treat this myself?		Find services/ experts	
Care and treatment at home	home	Treatment	healthfinder.gov

One of the most important things the classifications help you do is divide the list into smaller chunks. A longlist for a large Web site can be anything from 500 to 1,000 initial tasks. Even when you eliminate exact duplicates and words that are clearly irrelevant, you still might have between 400 and 500 tasks. That's an awful lot of stuff to go through. You will certainly have to run through the whole list a number of times in order to get a feel for it. However, trying to manage the entire list and bring it down to a shortlist is an almost impossible task. If you keep going through a very big list again and again, you run the risk of developing list blindness, so you should break the list up into chunks. That is what the Duplicate and Classification columns are for.

The following is a sample of what was classified as "Treatment" in the NHS Choices shortlist. By having the ability to focus only on the tasks in a particular class, you will be able to understand your list much better. You'll be able to really zone in and see things with greater clarity. And, of course, if you have misclassified something it should stand out from the rest of the tasks in that class.

Tasks	Duplicate	Class	Source
Appointment reminders		Treatment	
Book an appointment online		Treatment	
Can I get this on the NHS?		Treatment	
Care and treatment at home	home	Treatment	healthfinder.gov
Compare treatment options	options	Treatment	user goals doc
Cost of treatment		Treatment	CC health list
Description of operation/ procedure		Treatment	medlineplus.gov
Effects on my family		Treatment	NHSC
First Aid guide		Treatment	webmd.com

How do you develop the "Class"? You start by understanding your list. I rarely begin to add classes until I have gone through the list a number of times. Sometimes, a word in the longlist will actually lend itself to a class.

In an earlier version of the task list we had the phrase "healthy living". We ultimately deleted it from the list but we introduced a class called "Live well/healthy living". Here are some of the tasks we came up with in this classification:

- **Change your lifestyle (fitness, weight, smoking, drinking)**
- **Dealing with stress**
- **Diet, food and nutrition**
- **Find out how healthy you are**

Learn how others changed their lifestyle
Living with a condition/disease

GROUPING/AMALGAMATING TASKS

Next, we aim to reduce the number of items in the longlist by grouping them. For example, let's look at a task that ended up on the final NHS shortlist as "Diet, food and nutrition".

This task was actually the result of examining tasks such as:

Eat healthily
Food and nutrition
Food and recipes
Food and a condition/disease
Healthy nutrition guide
What to eat/not to eat

When do you amalgamate? When do you not amalgamate? Like much of the shortlisting process, it's not an easy decision. While assembling the longlist is relatively easy, making the decisions that bring you to a shortlist containing the range of tasks your customers wish to complete in language that is simple and clear is far from easy. Take as long as is necessary to get the shortlist right.

Remember that the actual words you choose for your tasks are incredibly important. When I worked with a consumer electronics company, we changed the words "Find a dealer" to "Buy/Shop locator" and doubled the amount of visitors to the online shop as a result. Sometimes you'll know amalgamation should occur but you'll still want to carry out tests to find the most powerful word. Thus, when I did the tourism task identification project I left in both of these tasks:

Deals
Special offers

These are in essence the same task but I wanted to know which resonated most with the customer. Based on my experience with many shortlists, I knew that I would ultimately amalgamate these words. "Special Offers" resonated far more than "Deals". This was particularly so within the European, Australian and New Zealand markets. However, in the United States, while "Special Offers" still got the biggest vote, "Deals" was not far behind.

An interesting thing to understand here is that practically nobody searches for "Special Offers", while millions search for "Deals". I have found over the years that the words people search with are often just a hint at what they really care about. They don't always tell the true and total story, and that's why you shouldn't exclusively depend on the words people use when they search to help you understand what their tasks are. (There are some good examples of this in the Microsoft Office case study in Chapter 10.)

The ideal task tends to be at level two of the classification—not too general and not too specific.

WHAT IS A TYPICAL TASK?

A typical task is what I would call a level two classification task. A level one classification task is what you will see on the homepage or in the classification at the top of the homepage on many Web sites. It's a classification like:

- About us
- Products

This is generally too big, too macro. It's not really a task, but rather a group of tasks. One way of checking if a task is too big and all-embracing is to ask yourself the following questions:

- **If this gets a big vote what are we going to do?**

- What things are we going to improve?
- What specific aspects of the Web site are we going to focus on?

At the other end, if you choose too many micro tasks it will be difficult to keep the shortlist under 100. Also, a particular micro task may not get a good vote because it is too specific. This sort of micro task is generally what I think of as level three or below. For the NHS Choices task identification we decided that the names of diseases and conditions (cancer, diabetes, etc.) would be too micro as tasks and that instead we should use task descriptions such as "Basic facts about a condition/disease". Another reason we did this was because, like the demographic-related tasks (women's health), disease-related tasks are only likely to get votes from those specifically interested in those particular diseases.

So, the ideal task tends to be at level two of the classification— not too general and not too specific. This, of course, is not always true—it's just a general rule. As you iterate through your task list, you will begin to get a feel for it and get a sense for its unity and wholeness. That's why it can take four to six weeks to get a longlist together and bring it to a shortlist. It's simply not something you can rush if you want to get it right.

What type of task words to use

Use task words that are clear, simple, and short. Use words that are roughly equal in their scope on the list. Consider the following two tasks:

- Diseases and conditions
- Healthy recipes

"Diseases and conditions" is really a major classification containing many tasks. "Healthy recipes" is a very specific task. You want your shortlist to feel unified, with all tasks roughly at the same level. Having some tasks that are incredibly micro and some tasks that are incredibly macro will cause problems, because:

- **it will make the list more difficult and confusing to scan;**
- **it will make the results more difficult to analyze and act upon.**

"Diseases and conditions" is too macro—too big. It's more like a class. So, we broke it up into a sub-set of tasks including the following:

- **Avoiding and preventing disease**
- **Basic facts about conditions/diseases**
- **Causes of a condition/disease**

We deleted "Healthy recipes" and included the following task, which we felt covered it and related tasks:

- **Diet, food and nutrition**

What type of task words not to use

1. Don't use words that are vague or overly technical.

2. Don't use abbreviations if possible. Or at least spell them out, and then put the abbreviations in brackets.

3. Don't use department names or organizational unit names.

4. Don't use application tool names. Rather, what does the tool help you to do?

5. Don't use brand names if possible. Put down the task the brand is supposed to help complete and put the brand name in brackets if necessary.

THE FINAL SHORTLIST

The final shortlist should be 100 tasks or fewer. We have experimented with lists of up to 150 and, amazingly, you will still get lots of people to vote and vote well. But you will certainly lose a number of people because of the list length. One hundred tasks is a very long list, and I know it shouldn't work; it breaks all the rules—but a significant number of people will vote on a list this long.

However, 100 is not an absolute and it's not mandatory. Smaller organizations will have smaller lists, but 100 tasks should be the limit because that's a lot of tasks. We have worked for some of the largest organizations in the world including Microsoft, Cisco, the United States Internal revenue Service, Schlumberger, IKEA ,and HSBC, and 100 tasks worked for them. And what's good about this limit of 100 is that it puts nice constraints on thinking.

In a world of endless choice there has never been a greater need to have constraints, rules, or limits. What we really need is quality thinking inside the box. We just need to choose the right box. Because we limited people to 100, they began to clarify what exactly constitutes a task, what should be amalgamated, what should be removed because it's a minor task. But who should these people be? Who should be involved in the shortlisting? In short, the experts and the people who matter.

STEPS IN FINALIZING THE SHORTLIST

Getting to the final shortlist is an iterative process. When the original longlist is about 500–600 terms, you need about five sessions lasting two to three hours each to examine and refine the list. In these sessions you should aim to include no more than five people. These people should have authority, experience, and a true feel and understanding for your customers.

As you bring the list under 200—preferably in the region of 150—it's of great use to take a number of experts (three to five, generally) through the list individually. Sit down with them and ask them to read over it. This will take about an hour. The following kinds of questions should be asked:

● **Are the tasks in the customer's language?**
● **Is there anything missing?**
● **Are there any duplicates that need to be merged?**

Make sure that the key stakeholders within your organization have had their say. These powerful people may have pet tasks. If possible, allow at least some of these tasks to remain on the list. Such pet tasks may well get a very small vote but that itself will prove a very important point. If the top task got 3,500 votes, and their pet task got 14 votes and is 98th in the list, there's an undeniable clarity about it. That sends a clear message.

The final shortlisting workshop is a very important event in the process. Its purpose is to finalize and sign off the shortlist. Keep the following in mind:

1. **Avoid including more than five people. The conversations can get intense and the more people involved, the longer it will take to get consensus.**

2. **Make sure, if at all possible, that anyone who attends the final workshop has been through an earlier version of the list at least once and is genuinely familiar with the process. Otherwise, you could spend a lot of time educating one person about the method and process and thus waste a lot of time.**

3. Schedule at least half a day. For intense and difficult lists, a final shortlisting workshop can often end up taking a whole day.

4. Try to have your longlist at 150 tasks or fewer before going into the workshop otherwise you may not get to the final list in that session.

AND THE TOP TASK FOR HEALTH IS…

"Check symptoms" is the top task on the NHS Choices Web site, whether you are a doctor or a patient, rich or poor, living in the North of England or the South, whether you have a short-term illness or a long-term one.

How to read the table opposite

Tasks: This column lists the tasks in order of their votes, with the task with the highest vote at the top.

Total Vote: This column gives the count of the vote each task received. "Check symptoms" got a total vote of 1,387.

% of Total Vote 30,255: This column expresses each vote as a percentage of the total votes cast, which in this situation was 30,255. So, "Check symptoms", with 1,387 votes, received 5% of the total votes.

Cumulative Vote: This column adds the percentage votes for the preceding tasks together. For 'Basic facts', it's 8%, which is the vote for "Basic facts" and "Check symptoms" added together. (There is rounding, so that total may vary slightly from the individual percentages.)

Cumulative Carewords: This column adds the percentages for the preceding carewords (tasks) together. There were 86 tasks voted on in this particular survey, so each task represents 1.2% of the total. Thus, the first four tasks represent 5% of the total tasks voted on.

Tasks	Total Vote	% of Total Vote 30255	Cumulative Vote	Cumulative Carewords
Check symptoms	1387	5%	5%	1%
Basic facts about conditions/diseases	1084	4%	8%	2%
Book an appointment online	1075	4%	12%	3%
Get advice from a doctor/nurse (phone, Web site chat, E-mail)	986	3%	15%	5%
What to do based on your symptoms	937	3%	18%	6%
Best place to go for help (GP, A&E, clinic, walk-in centre, pharmacist)	800	3%	21%	7%
When to seek urgent medical attention	694	2%	23%	8%
Get your medical records online	690	2%	25%	9%
How a condition/disease should be treated	670	2%	28%	10%
What to do in a medical emergency	624	2%	30%	12%
Get test results online	622	2%	32%	13%
Opening times (GPs, clinics, chemists)	570	2%	34%	14%
Can I treat this myself?	555	2%	35%	15%
Seriousness of a condition/disease (prognosis)	549	2%	37%	16%
Diet, food, and nutrition	539	2%	39%	17%
Compare hospitals based on quality of care (infection rates, MRSA, surgical errors, death rates)	531	2%	41%	19%
Contact details for hospitals, GPs, gyms, etc.	522	2%	42%	20%
Treating common health problems at home	515	2%	44%	21%
Choose a GP that's right for you	501	2%	46%	22%
Tips for coping with a condition/disease	499	2%	47%	23%

It's not a very Long Neck: 5% of the tasks get 15% of the vote, whereas we usually find that 5% of tasks get in the region of 25% of the vote. The top eight tasks got as much of the vote as the bottom 44, whereas usually the top five tasks get as much of the vote as the bottom 60. The top task, "Check symptoms", got 1,387 votes, whereas the bottom task, "Learn how others changed their lifestyle", got 59.

The following table shows that while the neck may not be as long as usual, it certainly is consistent. The chart takes a sample at 25%, 50%, 75%, and 100% of the vote. The top eight tasks that had emerged at 504 voters (25% of the vote) remained at the top for the rest of the vote.

Tasks	504 voters	1008 voters	1512 voters	2017 voters
Check symptoms	4%	5%	5%	5%
Basic facts about conditions/diseases	4%	3%	3%	4%
Book an appointment online	4%	3%	4%	4%
Get advice from a doctor/nurse (phone, Web site chat, E-mail)	3%	3%	3%	3%
What to do based on your symptoms	3%	3%	3%	3%
Best place to go for help (GP, A&E, clinic, walk-in centre, pharmacist)	3%	3%	3%	3%
When to seek urgent medical attention	2%	3%	2%	2%
Get your medical records online	2%	2%	2%	2%
How a condition/disease should be treated	2%	2%	2%	2%
What to do in a medical emergency	2%	2%	2%	2%
Get test results online	2%	2%	2%	2%
Opening times (GPs, clinics, chemists)	2%	2%	2%	2%
Can I treat this myself?	2%	2%	2%	2%
Seriousness of a condition/disease (prognosis)	2%	2%	2%	2%

Tasks	504 voters	1008 voters	1512 voters	2017 voters
Diet, food, and nutrition	2%	2%	2%	2%
Compare hospitals based on quality of care (infection rates, MRSA, surgical errors, death rates)	2%	2%	2%	2%
Contact details for hospitals, GPs, gyms, etc.	2%	2%	2%	2%
Treating common health problems at home	2%	2%	2%	2%
Choose a GP that's right for you	1%	2%	2%	2%
Tips for coping with a condition/disease	2%	2%	1%	2%

As you can see from the following table, "Check symptoms" was the top task for all professional categories:

Tasks	Health Prof	Higher Mgmt	Inter. Mgmt	Supervisory	Skilled Manual	Other Manual	Not in Work	Total
Check symptoms	4%	5%	5%	5%	6%	4%	3%	5%
Basic facts about conditions/diseases	3%	4%	5%	4%	4%	2%	3%	4%
Book an appointment online	3%	5%	4%	4%	3%	4%	3%	4%
Get advice from a doctor/nurse (phone, Web site chat, E-mail)	3%	3%	3%	4%	3%	4%	4%	3%
What to do based on your symptoms	3%	4%	4%	3%	3%	3%	2%	3%
Best place to go for help (GP, A&E, walk-in centre, pharmacist)	4%	2%	3%	3%	3%	2%	2%	3%

There were a few areas where "Check symptoms" was not the top task. It was fifth for males, with their top task being "Book an appointment online". The fourth task for males was, "Get medical records online", perhaps showing a greater desire for self-service and convenience among males than among females. For those over 55, "Check symptoms" was not the top task because, basically, they already know what they are dying of.

One of the most important lessons you must learn in managing a Web site is that you can't please everybody. There will always be people who do not want to complete the top tasks. That's just the way it is. However, exceptions don't mean that we should lose focus on what the majority need; making it easy for most people to complete their top tasks quickly and easily. There is an inevitable trade-off here, something that must be faced up to: You can't make everyone happy and you can't make every task easy to complete. Try to make everything easy and you make everything complicated.

IT WAS ONLY A STOMACH ACHE

So, "Check symptoms" is the top task for people who visit the NHS Choices Web site. Well, we tested a few "Check symptoms"— type tasks like "Stomach pain". The first search result read:

> **Real stories stomach cancer—Stomach cancer— Health A–Z**
> Deborah Knifton was devastated to find out that she had stomach cancer…They take your stomach away and attach the end of your lower bowel to…

Should that be the first result for "Stomach pain"? It's great to have real-life stories and blogs and the like. However, when someone types in a symptom do you really want to hit them with the most extreme example of what that symptom could represent? When you manage the tasks, rather than the content or the technology, you begin to see the world from the customer's point of view. And that world can look very different to how the organization sees it.

chapter 8

Free money: That's what we want

Cooperative trading between nonrelatives is a uniquely human activity. No other species has developed the combination of trading among strangers and a division of labor that characterizes the human economy.

Eric D. Beinhocker

GROWING A BUSINESS IN IRELAND

What sort of government support does a fast-growing Irish company with high export potential really want? That was the question that Enterprise Ireland, the government agency charged with supporting such companies, wanted answered. So, we started the process of identifying the tasks that companies with high-growth export potential wanted.

Here are the types of tasks we came up with:

Annual report for Enterprise Ireland	Book/find an event
Commercial funding sources (VC, seed, business angels)	Find Enterprise Ireland people (development, market, technical, legal)
Grants/equity funding from Enterprise Ireland (eligibility, description)	Innovation (guides, how-tos, networks)
Leadership/management development	News about Enterprise Ireland
Trade missions	Using IT in my business

We went out and got votes from 300 companies of the type Enterprise Ireland needs to support. The results are laid out in the following chart:

Tasks	Total	% of 3795	Cumulative Vote	Cumulative Words
Grants/equity funding from Enterprise Ireland (eligibility, description)	332	9%	9%	1%
Research and development funding	210	6%	14%	2%
Grants/equity funding online applications	205	5%	20%	4%
Market/competitor research	144	4%	23%	5%
Commercial funding sources (VC, seed, business angels)	128	3%	27%	6%
Market entry strategy advice	120	3%	30%	7%
Introductions to key industry decision makers/advisors	100	3%	33%	8%
EU funding for companies	99	3%	35%	10%
Find Enterprise Ireland people (development, market, technical, legal)	99	3%	38%	11%
Tax relief (BES, seed capital)	91	2%	40%	12%

So what's the top task? Grants and funding. Overwhelmingly so. Absolutely so. Grants and funding-type tasks are first, third, fifth, eighth, and tenth.

And there's certainly a Long Neck. The top 5% of the tasks get 23% of the vote. They get as much of the vote as the bottom 60%.

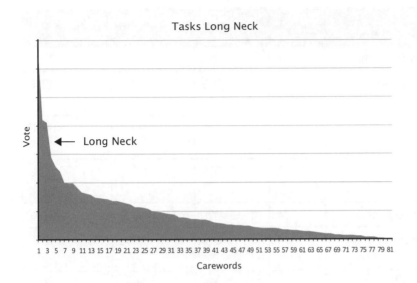

Tasks Long Neck

Carewords

And here's what was in the Long Tail:

Tasks	Total	% of 3795	Cumulative Vote	Cumulative Words
International logistics	13	0%	97%	77%
Design advice	12	0%	97%	78%
International legal issues (taxation, getting paid)	11	0%	98%	80%
Products/technologies available for licensing	10	0%	98%	81%
Translation and interpreting services	10	0%	98%	82%
Franchising	8	0%	98%	83%
Trade barriers for service companies	8	0%	99%	84%
Current Enterprise Ireland tenders	7	0%	99%	86%

Tasks	Total	% of 3795	Cumulative Vote	Cumulative Words
Irish economic profile summary	7	0%	99%	87%
Manage/change my event booking	7	0%	99%	88%
Annual report for Enterprise Ireland	6	0%	99%	89%
Enterprise Ireland's confidentiality policies	6	0%	100%	90%
Export duties and regulations	4	0%	100%	92%
Irish public sector purchasers' directory	4	0%	100%	93%
Purchasing policies for Enterprise Ireland	4	0%	100%	94%
Eolas as Gaeilge*	2	0%	100%	95%
Previous event presentations/ recordings	2	0%	100%	96%
Discuss/contribute to Enterprise Ireland's policies	0	0%	100%	98%
Freedom of Information Act	0	0%	100%	99%
Source Ireland	0	0%	100%	100%

* Information in Irish (Gaelic)

Out of 3,795 votes cast, not a single one went to "Discuss/ contribute to Enterprise Ireland's policies". "Annual report for Enterprise Ireland" got six votes out of 3,795.

GROWING A BUSINESS IN NORWAY

We were also asked to answer the same question by Innovation Norway. As we went through the longlisting and shortlisting process, we realized that the same types of tasks were emerging.

Over 900 Norwegian companies voted. Here are the top tasks that emerged (the list that was voted on was obviously in Norwegian, but we've translated it into English here).

Tasks	Total Vote	% of Total Vote 14055	Cumulative Vote	Cumulative Carewords
Grants	1037	7%	7%	1%
How to apply for funding	772	5%	13%	2%
Start-up grants	622	4%	17%	3%
Financing—how do I proceed	454	3%	21%	4%
Tax reduction	390	3%	23%	5%
Research and development contracts	362	3%	26%	6%
Innovation loans	323	2%	28%	7%
Business idea development tips	304	2%	30%	8%
Tourism campaigns	282	2%	32%	9%
Contact information (phone, E-mail etc.)	272	2%	34%	10%
Starting a business	268	2%	36%	11%
Loans and guarantees	267	2%	38%	12%
My pages (my application, loans etc.)	264	2%	40%	13%
Our services	245	2%	42%	14%
Focus area for Innovation Norway	239	2%	43%	15%
Templates (application, contracts etc.)	237	2%	45%	16%
High risk loans	230	2%	47%	18%
Business plan (templates, examples etc.)	229	2%	48%	19%
Our offices—Norway and abroad	227	2%	50%	20%
Sector news and trends	227	2%	52%	21%

And what was by far the top task? Grants and funding. Just like the Irish companies. And there's a definite Long Neck. As you can see from the chart, the top 5% of the tasks got 23% of the vote; mirroring the Irish trend.

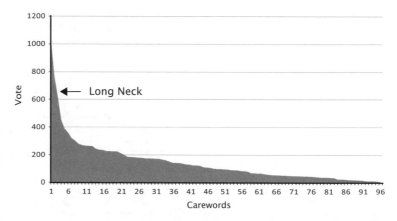

And here's the Long Tail:

Tasks	Total Vote	Total Vote	Cumulative Vote	Cumulative Carewords
Business set-up	42	0%	97%	80%
Competitor analysis	40	0%	97%	81%
Board candidates	39	0%	98%	82%
Search for a partner	39	0%	98%	84%
Loan calculator	37	0%	98%	85%
Intellectual property rights	35	0%	98%	86%
Export risk analysis	26	0%	98%	87%
Market key facts/numbers	26	0%	99%	88%
Internet bank (my loans)	25	0%	99%	89%
Annual report for Innovation Norway	22	. 0%	99%	90%
e-Learning	21	0%	99%	91%

Tasks	Total Vote	Total Vote	Cumulative Vote	Cumulative Carewords
Customer case studies	20	0%	99%	92%
IN consulting: How much does it cost?	19	0%	99%	93%
Corruption information	18	0%	100%	94%
Bankruptcy sales	14	0%	100%	95%
"The innovator" (the TV show)	13	0%	100%	96%
School collaboration	13	0%	100%	97%
Confidentiality agreements	12	0%	100%	98%
Post/E-mail records	9	0%	100%	99%
Project rooms on the Internet	1	0%	100%	100%

"Annual report for Innovation Norway" got 22 votes out of the 14,055 cast.

There was a category question in the Norwegian survey that asked companies to list the type of support they had recently received from Innovation Norway. Such support included consulting, networking, marketing, and, of course, funding and grants.

Struck by how strong the vote was for funding, Innovation Norway asked to see the difference if companies who had only selected funding were removed from the data. (The category question allowed respondents to select more than one type of support). The resulting top tasks were:

1. **Grants**

2. **How to apply for funding**

3. **Start-up grants**

4. Financing—how do I proceed?

Next, we were asked to remove companies that had selected funding as a type of support they had received from Innovation Norway, even though they had also selected other sources of support. And the top tasks were:

1. How to apply for funding

2. Grants

3. Start-up grants

4. Financing—how do I proceed?

So, the top task of those who hadn't yet received funding from Innovation Norway was how to apply for funding. Funding and grants are not just top tasks; they are super-tasks. They totally dominate, no matter how you analyze the data.

Embracing task management at Innovation Norway

Once Innovation Norway had identified their top tasks, they began to change the way they worked and how they were organized in order to truly create a task management environment, as the reality is that if people are not responsible for task success, then the model of task management can't work. There follows a table, created by Innovation Norway, that summarizes the journey they embarked upon in order to become more task-focused.

Before	After
Basic approach was: "We must show the users of our Web site absolutely everything we do and are"	The new content or page must prove that it supports a top task; that it is really needed by our customers
No focus on return on investment from the Web site	The Web site is treated as a business asset that must be managed professionally and show a return on investment
No forum for the management of the Web site	Task management forum established, meets weekly
Decentralized publishing: Writers could publish whatever they wanted	Centralized publishing: 100% control. Writers cannot publish directly
The only content that was truly managed was the news	From news to top task approach. Manage the tasks, not the content
No content review	All content must have a review date
Difficult to delete a page, check for broken links, etc.	Page deletion process is far more managed and streamlined
No testing	Continuous testing of top tasks, evolving the site, rather than big redesigns
Very little search management	Findability of top search words carefully managed
Metrics focused on number of visitors and number of times a page is viewed	Focus of metrics moves to task completion rates
Web team has 3.5 personnel	Web team has 4.5 personnel
Editorial workshops/courses were not that well thought through	Clear focus on customer-centric web writing. Workshops/courses are held two to four times a year

There follows a copy of the Innovation Norway homepage before the top task identification project.

1. The top of the page is dominated by an image. A translation of the text within the image reads: "We provide local ideas, global possibilities". This is the vision statement of Innovation Norway.

There now follows the new homepage. (This page is in beta as we go to print.) The top of the page is now dominated by the top tasks of funding and grants.

1. **Find funding and grants**

2. **Who qualifies?** What can you qualify for?

3. **What you can get?** What possibilities do the different grants provide?

4. **How do you apply?** Application forms, dates, and time schedules.

This new homepage is extremely practical and task-focused. Just what the customer wants.

GROWING A BUSINESS IN SCOTLAND

The Scottish Enterprise request was as follows: "Scottish Enterprise wants to better understand our customers' top tasks when visiting our Web site so that we can improve the support and services we provide to them." We went through the longlisting and shortlisting process and ended up with a list very similar to the one we had used for Enterprise Ireland and Innovation Norway. However, it was a bit shorter, with 66 tasks. The Enterprise Ireland list had 83 tasks and the Innovation Norway list had 97.

Two hundred and thirty Scottish companies voted. Here are the results.

Tasks	Total Vote	% of Total Vote 3420	Cumulative Vote	Cumulative Carewords
Am I eligible for grants/funding?	268	8%	8%	1%
Your industry, grants and funding	207	6%	14%	3%
How to apply for funding	155	5%	18%	4%
Leadership/management development	142	4%	23%	6%
Networking opportunities	132	4%	26%	7%
Marketing support, advice/programmes	117	3%	30%	9%
Other government funding/support	113	3%	33%	10%
Contract/tender opportunities (public sector)	108	3%	36%	12%
Innovation grants	96	3%	39%	13%
Research and development funding	95	3%	42%	15%
Support for managing high growth	88	3%	44%	16%
Productivity improvement advice/programmes	87	3%	47%	18%
Advice and expertise for your industry	86	3%	50%	19%
Who in Scottish Enterprise to contact	85	2%	52%	21%
News and trends in my industry	83	2%	54%	22%
Export my goods/services	75	2%	57%	24%
International networking to accelerate growth	68	2%	59%	25%
Apply online for grants or payments	67	2%	61%	27%
Contacts in Scottish Enterprise for my industry	67	2%	63%	28%
Market data and analysis (statistics etc.)	64	2%	64%	30%

And what was by far the top task? Grants and funding, of course. There's a Long Neck. The top 6% of tasks got 23% of the vote. Here's what the Long Neck looks like.

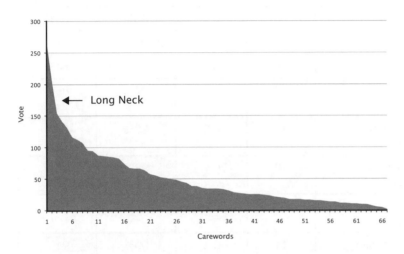

And here's what's in the Long Tail.

Tasks	Total Vote	% of Total Vote 3420	Cumulative Vote	Cumulative Carewords
List/profiles of Scottish Enterprise clients	21	1%	92%	69%
Best country to do business in for my industry	20	1%	93%	70%
How to become a Scottish Enterprise client	18	1%	93%	72%
Influence Scottish Enterprise's policy	18	1%	94%	73%
Product and service design and development	18	1%	94%	75%
About Scottish Enterprise	17	0%	95%	76%
Find a Scottish Enterprise office	17	0%	95%	78%

Tasks	Total Vote	% of Total Vote 3420	Cumulative Vote	Cumulative Carewords
Find an independent consultant/ professional advisor	16	0%	96%	79%
Import goods/services	16	0%	96%	81%
EU research opportunities	15	0%	97%	82%
License out my technology	14	0%	97%	84%
Online seminars/webinars/ podcasts	14	0%	97%	85%
Intellectual property (patent, trademarking, copyright)	12	0%	98%	87%
Test your idea (product establishment, market, etc.)	12	0%	98%	88%
Products/technologies available for licensing	11	0%	98%	90%
Research partner identification	11	0%	99%	91%
Collaborative research with other companies	10	0%	99%	93%
Manage/change my event booking	10	0%	99%	94%
Collaboration with third level researchers	8	0%	100%	96%
Investment deals Scottish Enterprise have made	6	0%	100%	97%
Organization chart for Scottish Enterprise	5	0%	100%	99%
Online foums (share ideas, ask for advice)	2	0%	100%	100%

So, not too many people are interested in "About Scottish Enterprise". Nor do too many want "Organization charts for Scottish Enterprise". They just want money—free money in the form of grants, preferably. Isn't that terrible? What has the world come to?

Customer top tasks often run up against cultural and image issues within the organization.

WHY WE LOVE THE GOVERNMENT

Governments do two basic things:

1. **They take money from us in the form of taxes**

2. **They give things back to us in the form of services**

Which do we prefer? It's getting money back, isn't it? So, when an entrepreneur or company looks at a government agency that is there to support them in starting up or growing, it's perfectly understandable that they would want to know how much money they can get. Grants would be the first choice, because grants are free. But other funding is also attractive, whether it is in the form of low interest loans or some sort of equity stake.

Believe me, I should understand this. I was—and I suppose still am—that sort of entrepreneur. One of the companies I founded during the dot com boom of the late 90s was fast-growing, high-profile, and export-focused. We got various forms of funding from Enterprise Ireland, and it was much appreciated.

The fact that someone comes to a government Web site and the first thing they want to know is if there are grants they can avail of does not automatically make them a bad person. Highly ambitious entrepreneurs with high-growth potential have that same question on their mind: Am I eligible?

Another interesting trend surfaced when we got staff within Enterprise Ireland and Innovation Norway to vote. We asked them to choose what they thought clients really wanted. And there was a huge consensus: Funding and grants. So, there's agreement on all sides. And, thus, the Web sites of all these agencies must have really easy-to-use grants and funding sections because it is such an overwhelming top task, right?

Well, not exactly. It turns out that "grants and funding" is not so simple a task after all. Partly, it's to do with the complexity of the situation. You will never be able to go to a government Web site, fill out a form and find grant money in your account the next day. You're going to have to meet someone, discuss and present plans, and then get approved.

Okay, then you can't get the grant or funding online. But the question that came up again and again as we talked to entrepreneurs in Norway, Ireland, and Scotland was: Am I eligible? They wanted to be able to go to the Web site and quickly—quickly being the operative word here—find out what grants and funding they were eligible for.

So, that should be easy to do, shouldn't it? Well...

Customer top tasks often run up against cultural and image issues within the organization. "We're more than just an entity that hands out money," the organization justifiably says. "We've got expert advisors. We guide young entrepreneurs and help open up export markets for companies that want to grow." And that's true.

But sometimes organizational issues run even deeper than that; organizations can be guilty of a type of fear or risk avoidance. The fear is that if you make the grants and funding section really easy, there will be a deluge of applications from companies that have no hope of ever getting funded. That will be a big waste of time. The problem is that by making the task more difficult to complete for those you don't want to help, you are also making it more difficult to complete for those you do want to help. We should not manage our Web sites based on the desire to keep certain groups away. Rather, we should focus on the top tasks of our top customers.

If by making it easy for our top customers to complete their top tasks we also make it easy for those we don't want to deal with, well, that's just the price of doing business. Because if we don't make it easy for those we need to do business with, we risk losing their business, and that is a higher price to pay.

And there's something else. Organizations employ people to help customers complete tasks offline. If the customers can complete these tasks online, then maybe the organization doesn't need as many employees. Sometimes tasks are made deliberately mysterious and complex because that indicates that the staff member who is helping the customer complete the task is doing a complex job and is thus a valuable employee. The Web – when it works—is disruptive of traditional organizational structures. A really successful Web site will change how the organization works and how it is staffed.

If you want time with your customers you need to prove that it will result in real gains.

THE AUTOMATION OF INFORMATION TASKS

Our history and folk songs are full of stories about the valiant woodcutters who fought against the chainsaw, and the railway builders who fought against the pump hammer. I remember hearing a story about Irish painters who went on strike when the paint roller was introduced. And when computers were first introduced in newspaper rooms, journalists were not allowed to type their own stories—the typesetter had to do it. Terrence Deal, author of many books on leadership and organizations, says, "Change is like a trapeze—you have to let go before you can move on." There has always been a natural resistance to the technology that replaces manual labor. But what is so valiant about inefficiency? Tasks that get automated are often routines or drudgery that people no longer think deeply about, or verbalize well, or measure accurately.

The automation of tasks requires a direct understanding or observation of those tasks. One of the biggest weaknesses that web teams have is that they don't understand their customers.

The Web is not some back-end IT activity, it's a customer-facing, task-focused one. It's not about writing code and servicing machines, but about observing people so that you can serve them better or, more importantly, allow them to serve themselves.

Web teams need to be out front, not back-office. And that's another organizational challenge (to be overcome). The web teams that actually do want to interact with their customers in order to identify their top tasks and make those tasks easy to complete are often actively blocked by other members of the organization.

I dealt with a large organization whose sales reps did not want to let the web team next to or near their customers. They claimed that the customer was sick and tired of being contacted by the organization, and that the Web was silly anyway—it had nothing to do with real sales. This was, it must be said, a business-to-business company that sold very expensive equipment.

But when we finally did get in touch with the customers, many of them didn't have a major problem helping. In fact, quite a few had loads of suggestions in relation to how the Web site could better serve their needs. The more we investigated, the more we discovered that the customers loved the technical detail the Web site delivered. (It was quite a good Web site.) More than one customer told me that before the Web he'd have to ring up his sales contact and ask for the technical detail. Now he could go to the Web and get it himself. He liked that. The sales reps, on the other hand, didn't. It was shifting power, undermining them.

In other organizations, I found sales reps who were delighted that the Web site was answering basic questions, because this gave them more time to deal with the complex issues that their customers had. So, this is not some rant about those nasty sales reps. It is true that change is hard and can be undermining and it is also true that, in many organizations, the Web has not yet fully proved itself. If you want time with your customers you need to prove that it will result in real gains.

chapter 9

Organization v.
customer thinking

*Science is a long history of learning
how not to fool ourselves.*

Richard Feynman

ELECTION WEB SITE TOP TASKS

If you visited the John McCain election Web site around May 2008, you would have been greeted by the following tasks on the first page:

- **Donate today**
- **E-mail sign-up**

No high-blown political language, just simple action-talk. If you visited the Barack Obama Web site at around the same time you would have seen one task on the first page:

- **Join the movement (E-mail sign-up)**

If you visited the Hillary Clinton Web site at around the same time you would also have seen one task on the first page:

- **Sign up as a supporter**

The top task is the same on all three Web sites: Make it easy for people to sign up to help the candidate get elected. But if your customer's top task is the same top task that your competitor's customers have, what should you do? Differentiate? Not put this top task on your homepage because your competitors already have it on their homepages and you want to be different? Not a good idea. Your response should be to seek to make it an easier, faster, better task completion experience than those of your competitors.

HOW DO YOU BUY A CAR?

Even when organizations know what their customers want and try to give it to them, they often use the wrong language. That's a big mistake on the Web.

The first step in using the right language on your Web site is identifying your customer's vocabulary. What's the most important thing to you when you're buying a new car? We asked a group of consumers that question in 2007. We gave them a list of about 90 tasks/factors including the following:

Accessories	Affordability
Big trunk	Brand reputation
Engine	Low fuel consumption
Price	Reliability ratings
Safety rating	Trunk capacity

The top four factors got 26% of the vote. They were as follows:

Affordability	**7%**
Price	**7%**
Low fuel consumption	**6%**
Safety rating	**6%**

We also tested about 40 "branding" statements. The question was: "Please look at the following list and choose the top three most important things you expect from a car company." The list included the following:

A company that cares about its customers	Beautiful design, simple operation
Excellent price/quality ratio	Great value for money
Incredibly fine design	Innovative
Quality and service	Reliable
State-of-the-art	Trustworthy brand

Two branding statements got 27% of the vote. These two statements got more of the vote than the bottom 34 in the list. They were:

Quality and service	15%
Excellent price/quality ratio	11%

We also asked people in the survey what their gender was. The top four factors for males and females were:

Rank	Female	Male
1	Affordability	Affordability
2	Price	Price
3	Safety rating	Quality
4	Low fuel consumption	Low fuel consumption

So, there was almost an exact match between what men and women wanted in a new car, the exception being that "Safety rating" was third for women, whereas "Quality" was third for men. The branding Long Neck statements were an exact match.

CUSTOMER CENTRIC V. ORGANIZATION CENTRIC

We then asked product managers and marketing people from a car manufacturer the following questions:

- What are the most important things to **your customers** when buying a new car?
- What are the most important things **your customers** expect from a car company?

What the manufacturer thought were the top factors influencing a customer's buying decision were as follows:

Design/style	10%
Quality	10%
Brand reputation	8%

While these factors were important to the customer ("Design/ style" was ninth, "Brand reputation" was eighth, and "Quality" was seventh), they were not part of the Long Neck.

The branding Long Neck for the car manufacturer was:

A company that cares about its customers	15%
Quality and service	14%

There is some crossover here. "Quality and service" resonates strongly with both groups. "A company that cares about its customers", while first for the car manufacturer, was fifth for the customer group. Not a bad match.

We dug into the data a bit more and identified the words and phrases that were statistically most important to each group. The following table shows the results.

More Important to Customer	More Important to Company
Reliability/ratings	Engine
Low fuel consumption	Design/style
Dependable	Quality
Affordability	Brand reputation

The left column tells us the story of customer centric, the right of organization centric. Engines, design, style and brand reputation are close to the hearts of those who work for car manufacturers. But what customers really care about is reliability, low fuel consumption, and affordability.

Those of us involved in Web sites need to accept that our core mindset is organization centric. The engine—the tool—fascinates. The design, style and brand are magnetic in their attraction. These are important things, for sure, but we must never allow them to obscure our view of how our customers see the world. Our Web sites must maintain a relentless focus on our customers' basic needs. We must understand that our customers are strangers to us. They are not our friends and they do not want to be our friends. We must make a daily effort to understand and stay in touch with their needs. If we don't, all the traditional marketing and promotion efforts in the world will be of diminished value.

FRAMING THE TASK INTRODUCTION QUESTION

Framing the question that introduces the task list is an important activity. Before we get into the essence of the question, let's look at the mechanics of what we want the person to do. We want them to scan the list quickly, choose their top five tasks, and then vote, giving their top task five points, their next top task four points, and so on. Here's the way we usually structure the question:

> **Please look at the following list and choose ONLY the top FIVE tasks that are of most relevance to you.**
> **Give a score of five to the task MOST IMPORTANT to you, four to the next most important, then three, two, and one.**
> **Please give ONLY one score of 5, one 4, one 3, one 2, and one 1. Leave the rest blank.**
> **Please trust your first instincts and spend no more than five minutes on this exercise.**

The first sentence changes depending on the project, but the remaining sentences are usually standard.

Below are examples of these first sentences:

1. Please look at the following list and choose ONLY the top FIVE most important things to you when deciding to buy a new car.

2. What five factors are most important to you when using a health Web site? Please look at the following list and choose ONLY the top FIVE factors that are of most relevance to you.

3. Please look at the following list and choose ONLY the top FIVE topics that are of most relevance to your business on the Enterprise Ireland Web site.

4. Below is a list of typical IT-related challenges that organizations face. Choose the top FIVE challenges you face for which you would consider looking for support from an external company.

5. Select the FIVE words or phrases from the following list that reflect the most important things to you in relation to a satellite navigation system.

We generally try to keep the first sentence more about the customer and their needs rather than the Web site or the organization. In Example three we did put the focus on the Enterprise Ireland Web site, but generally we advise against this, as some of the tasks on the list may not actually be on the Web site. Also, we want the person filling out the survey to focus on the tasks they want to complete, rather than the Web site itself.

With the NHS Choices question (Example two) we did refer to health Web sites, but in a general way and without specifying the NHS Choices Web site in particular. Example four was for

Microsoft Pinpoint and was neither organization nor Web site-specific. The same is true for Example five, which was for a consumer electronics company but didn't mention the company's name or the Web site.

As a general rule, frame the question from the customer's point of view. Always think of what's important to your customers. In this context, the name of the organization and the fact that it is doing something on a Web site is not that important. What is important is to focus your customers on identifying what really matters to them.

chapter 10

How the Microsoft Excel Web site dramatically improved customer satisfaction

Those who are most likely to make unbiased cognitive assessments are the clinically depressed.

Jon Elster

COMPLEXITY IS GOOD

Complex societies are successful and prosperous. Simple societies are poor and backward. New York is a complex place. The opposite of New York is a tiny village in an impoverished country that must supply all its own food and other goods. The villagers live a very simple life.

When most people talk about simplicity they're not thinking of subsistence. They want all the nice things a complex world can give them without the hassles and the pressures. The challenge is to deliver on the multitude of benefits that complex societies can offer, while minimizing the drawbacks of complexity. The complexity should sit in the background, doing all sorts of complex things that make life better. When all goes well, people live interesting, stimulating, productive, and varied lives and there are lots of quality choices. Time doing humdrum, labor-intensive tasks is greatly reduced and life is easier. It's a complex engine with a simple interface.

If any company has proven that complexity can yield numerous benefits, it's Microsoft. Software is, by its very nature, complex and Microsoft has reveled both in software variety and complexity and in a massive partnership ecosystem that supports and enhances this core software. Apple, on the other hand, has followed the path of simplicity and done very well too. But Microsoft's web of complexity has delivered a greater variety of products, lower prices, and a substantially greater market share.

I love Apple products. I have an iPod and the first computer I owned was an Apple Mac. But when I started a company, we bought PCs. The reasons for this were price and software variety and flexibility. If you made the effort to deal with the PC's complexity, you were able to get a lot more for your money. And when you're starting a company with practically zero financing, upfront cost is important.

To achieve simplicity, Apple embraced control. Is Apple's resurgence a sign that we have reached a complexity tipping point? That our world has become so cluttered, unfocused and overblown that the cost of dealing with its complexity is greater than the potential benefits?

Giving control of a Web site to a content author is a bit like giving a pub to an alcoholic.

TEN MILLION PAGES AND COUNTING

I have heard it said that there are roughly 10 million pages on the Microsoft Web site. Nobody really knows for sure—which tells a story in and of itself—but that is an agreed-upon estimate. Of those 10 million pages, some three million have never been visited by a human being. That's pretty much half the population of Ireland in webpages that nobody has ever visited. It would not be wildly unreasonable to ask why Microsoft created these pages in the first place.

Back in 2002 I had lunch with a Microsoft executive. I told them that they really needed to focus on content quality, and that they needed to implement review processes for the content they had already published. He looked at me as if I were an innocent lad from Ireland who didn't quite get it when it came to managing large Web sites. He politely informed me that Microsoft had lots of really smart people and that the future of Web site management was about giving these really smart people good publishing tools, and then getting out of the way.

What that Microsoft executive was telling me was really not very different from what most executives in large and small organizations had been telling me. Web site management was about distributed publishing, distributed control—a hands-off approach. It was about releasing the genius author inside everyone within the organization.

Sometime in 2005 I got a call from another Microsoft manager who told me that Microsoft was now suffering from "extreme content proliferation". The model of letting everybody publish whatever they wanted whenever they wanted hadn't worked very well.

The reality is that giving control of a Web site to a content author is a bit like giving a pub to an alcoholic. It's happy days. All that stuff that couldn't be published in print—including all the stuff that *could* be published in print—can now be easily put up on the Web. Inevitably, it leads down the road of ruin.

Having a 10-million-page Web site is something you should admit at a WWW meeting. (That's the Web equivalent to an AA meeting.)

"Hi. I'm Gerry. I have a 10-million-page Web site."

"Hi, Gerry."

"I used to have a one-million-page Web site, but I had no self-control. It was just one more page, one more page…"

"We know. We know…"

A different kind of analysis is needed that is not focused on the volume of pages or the volume of visitors.

ONCE UPON A TIME THERE WAS A WEB SITE…

Once upon a time there was a Web site, and a very good Web site it was. It had high hopes and lofty ambitions. It had a vision to:

- **"Give your customers what they want"**
- **"Help them find what they need"**

The web team took this vision and quickly turned it into a simple objective:

Publish lots of cool content.

They started publishing lots and lots of pages. Things were good: Page views were increasing and the manager encouraged them to publish more good pages. "We can do better," the manager said. So the web team focused on publishing more, better, faster. They had become the quintessential Web team and it felt good.

Time went by. A pattern developed. It was all about publishing. The Web site grew and so did the number of visitors. At one level, the Web site was really successful. It had lots of visitors and lots of page views, and that looked like success. And that was what was communicated to management. "We have lots of visitors and lots of page views. Everything is increasing. Things are good."

But then someone came to the web team with a different way of analyzing success. They did a different kind of analysis that is not focused on the volume of pages or the volume of visitors. This analysis is based on finding out whether customers are satisfied or not; whether they are able to complete the tasks they came to the Web site to complete. It turned out that customers were not satisfied. They complained about how "It's not what I want", and "I can't find it", and "I don't like it".

The web team was taken aback. All this hard work and the customers were still not satisfied. How could that be? They shook their heads and decided to redouble their efforts in order to find a solution.

They figured that some of the problems must be associated with the content that was already on the Web site, so they decided to revise and improve it.

They reckoned that another problem was that their customers couldn't find the right pages. So they decided to really optimize their Web site for search engines. They added lots and lots of keywords to every page; lots and lots. They worked hard on the title tags to make them keyword rich.

Then they thought that another reason for customer dissatisfaction was the links. So they decided to redesign the navigation and add more links. Links like "See more" and "Related links" and "Buy this", and "No, really, you need to see this", and "You might even be interested in this". And they added these links to the homepage and sub-homepages and to document pages, and to any pages they could find. It was hard work but they felt good after all this effort to help the customer. Because they really do want to help the customer. Their hearts are in the right place.

Surely all this effort would lead to increased customer satisfaction. The team waited excitedly to hear.

We are managers of our customers' time as they seek to complete tasks.

PRODUCTION IS KING

We live in a world where production is glorified. There is a cult of volume. For millions of years it has been about how many cows you owned, how many acres of land you had, how much your factory could produce, how many lines of content or code you could write. Those who produce have value; those who don't, don't. Productivity is the essence of capitalism—it's all about producing more stuff with fewer people. It's deeply ingrained in management thinking; it's in the genes.

We solve problems. If it ain't broke we don't fix it. We are inherently and naturally reactive and project driven. We are launch-and-leave cultures. It's about the new and the next. There is nothing cool or positive about continuous improvement of something that already exists. The hero invents the new, creates something that nobody has ever thought of before.

That which makes us stronger can kill us in the end. The rules of the physical world do not apply in quite the same way in the digital world. The world of atoms is not the world of information. We're like a T-Rex sitting in a classroom being told to pay attention, to stop looking out the window. This T-Rex is being told that the future is about mammals. So, the T-Rex shrugs a fatalistic shrug, pushes the seat back, jumps up, and eats the teacher.

The beauty of human beings is we are not forced to follow an inevitable path. We can, with enough effort, retrain our brains and put a brake on the drives of our genes. We don't have to listen to that incessant voice that says "produce, reproduce, consume, produce, reproduce, consume."

We live in a digital world, a world of content. However, most organizations are totally unprepared and unwilling to manage content professionally. The Web is seen as an "IT problem". Perhaps it is seen as a communications challenge.

Sure, it's a challenge and that's why it's so exciting to be around right now. We are realizing that we should not be managing technology or content, but rather our customers' experience as they seek to complete a task. It is not organizational productivity that we should focus on (unless we're managing an intranet). Rather, it is customer productivity that should monopolize our attention. Customers are spending their time on our Web sites and the best thing we can do is help them waste as little time as possible. We are managers of our customers' time as they seek to complete tasks.

One of the most important things to manage is dissatisfaction with a specific task

THE CUSTOMER IS DICTATOR

The aforementioned web team had done all the things that quality web teams have been trained to do in order to make the Web site better. They had worked on and revised the pages; they had added lots of links and keywords. This was a genuine effort to make things better. Many web teams would have done nothing at all to the pages that already existed; they would simply have kept publishing new pages.

It didn't work. Things didn't get any better. For all that web publishing work, customer satisfaction remained flat. And the Web site had grown larger and was now even harder to maintain. What to do?

At least the web team now has the right metrics. It measured the satisfaction of customers who have tried to complete tasks on its Web site. Not general satisfaction, but satisfaction with a particular task. Most Web sites are measured—if they are measured at all—on extremely crude and often totally misleading measures such as the volume of visitors and pages. These truly negative and misleading measures actually encourage worst practice on the Web—the production of lots and lots of pages. So, this web team is way ahead of most web teams. But they are still stuck in a rut.

The web team in question is the Microsoft Office Content Publishing group that manages the Office.com site, and one of their focus areas is the Excel content pages. They needed a breakthrough, a new way of working, and this breakthrough came when they realized that one of the most important things to manage is **dissatisfaction** with a specific task. "It is not sufficient to only work towards increasing satisfaction," states Maya Subramanian, business development and strategies analyst. "In fact, lowering dissatisfaction is more critical."

Instead of only measuring satisfaction with a task, why not also measure dissatisfaction? Why not quantify all the people who were unable to complete their tasks when they came to the Web site and try to identify what it was that caused them to fail? It's one thing to show how many people completed the task because of a particular piece of content, but how many people were confused by the content and unable to complete the task as a result? And, just as importantly, did this piece of content hurt the completion of other more important tasks?

The team established two basic objectives:

1. **Publish more satisfactory pages, and seek to increase page views of these satisfactory pages.**

2. **Remove dissatisfactory pages, and if they can't be removed, minimize their findability.**

Every time you add, you add complexity.

JOHAN FROM LITHUANIA

Never underestimate the ability of some people to ignore the blatantly obvious and instead spot and fervently defend the utterly obscure. Web management should be first and foremost about establishing general rules, and then and only then, dealing with the exceptions. If you manage based on exceptions you will drive yourself to despair and your Web site to ruin.

"You can't delete that!"

"Why not?"

"Johan needs it."

"Johan who?"

"Johan from Lithuania."

"Who?"

"Johan from Lithuania who's married to Isabelle from Italy and who's just broken both his legs. He needs that content. We have to keep that page up for Johan."

There is something in us that is attracted to the unusual. I suppose we become bored with the ordinary. Maybe we assume that the frequently asked question was answered well enough already. But the infrequently asked question, ah, now that's a challenge. And shouldn't our purpose be to answer all questions, to not leave Johan out in the cold?

The Web is littered with good intentions. There is a webpage that answers—or at least attempts to answer—every question that was ever asked, and many that weren't. And this is the crux of the matter. How do you manage all this stuff? How do you make sure it works, that it helps people solve tasks? How do you keep it up to date?

There is an even greater problem. Every time you add, you add complexity. Adding the answer to one question can make it harder for someone to find the answer to another. As the volume of content increases so too does the complexity, and the magic search engine will not always sort it out. Let's say your Web site has answers for questions A, B, C, D, and E. Question A gets 80% of the demand. Question E has a somewhat similar title to Question A, but has a very different answer. So 20% of the people who want an answer to Question A end up on the page for Question E. They get the wrong answer and they leave very frustrated.

Did you hear about the death of the Frequently Asked Question (FAQ)? If you remember the Web from the early days, then you might remember that the FAQ was everywhere. It's largely extinct now, and I think I know why.

The FAQ was diligent, upright, honest, and hard working (if somewhat balding). One night it was walking home from work. It was late, as usual. It was dark and it was raining, and the FAQ had to pass through an unsavory part of town. Suddenly, it was grabbed from behind, dragged down an alley and beaten to death by a bunch of good-for-nothing infrequently asked questions. That's what happened to the Frequently Asked Question.

As the causes of dissatisfaction at Microsoft Excel were investigated it became clear that some content was just getting in the way.

TIME TO LET GO

It's hard to let content go; to send it into retirement. In fact, it doesn't seem right. It's not intuitive and it's rarely rewarded, either. At Microsoft—as with practically all organizations I have worked with—the mechanism of reward is geared towards those who create, code, write, launch, ship, and publish. We produce things. We're human. It's hard to accept that on the Web we're in the business of service, of solving problems. It's much easier to see our jobs as creators of content rather than solvers of problems.

After a lot of discussion, the team decided to launch an effort called "Weeding the Garden". "Organizations need to understand that 'weeding' is work," says Laurel Hale, Excel content publishing manager. "It takes time to weed intelligently with the best interests of the customer in mind. Therefore, content publishing managers need to allocate time in their schedules for this valuable work."

As the causes of dissatisfaction at Microsoft Excel were investigated it became clearer and clearer that some content was just getting in the way. But the idea of actually deleting that content was a really hard concept for the web team to accept. Some had never deleted before and didn't even know how to go about it.

There were lots of arguments for keeping content. "I'm sure some users still use it!" was one. Yes, you will always find a Johan if you look hard enough. But what happens when far more people actually hate the content, when far more people find that the content not only doesn't solve their problem but sends them in the wrong direction, and stops them from getting to the right content?

"Taking things away isn't the right thing to do. We should fix them." Some things should never have been published in the first place. If there's something wrong with a page it should be fixed or removed. It's not good enough to say you'll get to it. Fix it now or take it down. It's important to understand that poor-quality content is worse than no content. If you give someone the wrong directions there's no point in saying: "Well, at least I gave them *some* directions."

"OK, they aren't useful, but certainly there's no harm in just leaving them there?" Oh yes there is. Old content builds up over time. If you are not regularly reviewing and removing, the amount of out-of-date content will grow and grow, making it increasingly difficult to find fresh and useful content.

Do you go to the cinema looking for the four-hour films? Sure you do. Because those four-hour films are twice the value of the two-hour films. And we all know it's so much better value to buy 900-page books. Haven't you figured that out yet? Those 300-page books are €20, while 900-page books are €40. Do they think I'm a fool!? I know I get far better value per page if I buy bigger books.

Customers see content from a totally different perspective to content producers. They don't seek out content in volume. They don't think a site is good just because it has lots of content, it has to have the right content. "Our original team agreement was to remove or expire pages as a first resort, so we looked at the traffic patterns and customer feedback to figure out what was happening," says Laurel Hale. This took courage and a lot of convincing, because removing content was anathema to the Microsoft culture.

WHAT WE SEARCH FOR IS NOT ALWAYS WHAT WE NEED

Lots of people were searching for "Remove conditional formatting". So, it was decided to publish a dedicated page called "Remove conditional formatting", which explained exactly how to remove conditional formatting.

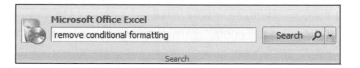

However, this new page "Removing conditional formatting" began getting a lot of customer dissatisfaction ratings. So the web team revised it. Still lots of dissatisfaction. On the surface, the page looked fine. The information was clear and well-written. However, as Laurel explains, "Many customer comments for the 'Removing conditional formatting' article indicated that they weren't really looking just for removing conditional formatting, but really needed to figure out how to use the feature—how to apply it, how to remove it (yes), and how to change conditional formatting once it was applied—most likely this is what led them to search for how to remove it. Sometimes customers look for one thing, but really need something else, or something more."

Sometimes, the words people use in search are just a hint at what they really need. They may end up on the wrong page because of the words they have chosen. If you don't do your research properly, you could draw some false and damaging conclusions:

1. **This term is being searched for a lot. Therefore we need a page for it.**

2. **This page is being found a lot in search. Therefore we need to keep it.**

3. **Actually, what we need to do is create even more pages like this, and that will mean we'll get found in search more.**

There was a page on the Excel site called "Format text in a variety of ways based on conditions". This page had the comprehensive help Microsoft customers needed, including applying, removing, and changing conditional formatting. So the team deleted the topic "Removing conditional formatting" and optimized search for the overall page. The result? People were now much more likely to find the comprehensive topic (misleading choices had been removed). Satisfaction increased and dissatisfaction decreased.

BAD LINKING LEADS TO RUIN

Linking is the essence of what makes the Web the Web. There is no more important skill for a web writer to have. Linking involves thinking about customer tasks and journeys. Where do customers want to go and what's the best way to get them there? As with everything, too much linking leads to confusion. Giving a person a wrong—or badly worded—link is like giving a driver bad directions. You will waste their time and make them very annoyed.

One of the early initiatives from the Excel team was to add lots more links to the pages. This clearly wasn't working and they realized they needed to take a quality, not quantity, approach to link writing. As a result of studying customer behavior, the Excel team noticed some interesting patterns. Lots of customers were searching for help on Excel PivotTables. They'd get to the page on Excel PivotTables. On the page was a "See also" heading, below which was the following link:

Ten tutorials about creating PivotTable reports for Excel Services

Some things you need to know about the above link:

1. **PivotTables in Excel Services is very different to Excel. If you're interested in PivotTables in Excel, these tutorials will be of no help.**

2. **Most people don't know there is such a thing as Excel Services or that it's quite different from Excel.**

3. **People scan on the Web. They read only as much as they need to. The link that most of them actually see and click is:**

Ten tutorials about creating PivotTable

When you are writing for the Web, always start with the most important words. Lead with the need. Begin with the essence of the message; the most important element. In the original link the most important element is Excel Services. The tutorials are for Excel Services, not Excel, so we should start with Excel Services. And, of course, an even more important point is whether people would know the difference anyway. A great many people might think that Excel Services are services connected with the Excel spreadsheet program. This is a classic example of how the language used to describe the tiny task (Excel Services), impacts on the ability to complete the top task (Excel).

"They see a link to this topic, and go there," Laurel explains, "only to realize this topic is about Excel server, not Excel, and get very, very mad at us! So we removed the 'See also' link to this topic from the general PivotTable topics. We also removed it from the Excel Table of Contents. And what was the result? Page views fell by over 77%. Dissatisfaction fell by over 15%."

Home> Products> Excel> Excel 2007 Help and How-to

PivotTable reports and PivotChart reports

Ten tutorials about creating PivotTable reports for Excel Services

By taking a top tasks approach, many of the pages saw a satisfaction increase of 15% or more.

HIDING PAGES FROM SEARCH

Sometimes getting found is not a good thing. Particularly if what's getting found has been found instead of what should have been found.

"The Excel Function Reference was notorious for generating dissatisfaction," Laurel states. "We couldn't remove these pages because they are mapped to the user interface for the product. We started looking at customer feedback and realized that the wrong customers were finding these topics. For example, English teachers, who wanted to add numbers were finding the IMSUM function. Administrative assistants, who wanted to print address labels, were finding the ADDRESS function. Students, who wanted to set the print area, were finding the AREAS function."

So, the Excel team deleted all the individual function pages, bringing them all together into a single page called "Math functions". "When customers searched for 'sum numbers'," Laurel explains, "the basic topic appeared at the top of the search results." And instead of seeing another search result called "IMSUM function", they would instead see a search result called

"Math functions" and not click it. Of course, the experts who needed these math functions would understand the title of the result and click it.

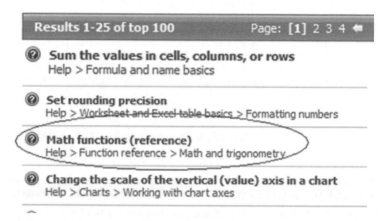

Searched for: "sum numbers"

So, managing the Long Neck—making it easier to complete top tasks—does not always have to make it more difficult to complete tiny tasks. By clearly directing people to the top tasks of sum numbers, set print areas, and print address labels, and keeping them away from the function topics, the dissatisfactory usage of the function topics dramatically decreased. "Dissatisfactory function reference page views decreased by 42%," Laurel explains. "Satisfactory page views increased by 423%!" That's impressive.

This is Microsoft. And it's not about technology, it's about psychology. What the Microsoft Excel team achieved is at heart based on a better understanding of their customers. This is not a technological issue, but rather a human one. In an age where more and more is done with the aid of technology, it has never been more important to understand how people behave as they interact with this technology and what their true needs are.

The Excel team "weeded" 50% of the Excel pages. "Six months before weeding, approximately 10% of all page views were dissatisfactory," Laurel confirms. "Six months after weeding, dissatisfactory page views dropped to barely 3% of total page views." For years, satisfaction with many pages on Excel had remained under 50%. By taking a top tasks approach, many of the pages saw a satisfaction increase of 15% or more. That's pretty dramatic.

LESSONS LEARNED

According to Maya Subramanian, the key lessons learned were:

- **You can't succeed by tending to satisfaction alone. You must also focus on reducing dissatisfaction.**
- **Ongoing weeding is crucial. Running a Web site is a process of continuous improvement. It is not about launch and leave.**
- **Cross-team collaboration is a must for success. Helping customers solve tasks nearly always requires cooperation across teams, departments, and silos. No one group can do it all.**
- **Customers don't notice when poor pages vanish or when they become harder to find. But they certainly do notice when poor pages are easy to find. And they really, really hate them.**
- **The Excel team ended up with fewer pages to manage, which means they have more time to invest in the continuous improvement of top tasks.**

chapter 11

A method for managing search

Instinctive cooperativeness is the very hallmark of humanity and what sets us apart from other animals.

Matt Ridley

PSYCHOLOGY, NOT TECHNOLOGY

Helping people find things means understanding the task they wish to complete. As we saw in the previous chapter, you can't simply take the search terms people use at face value. Lots of people search for "Remove conditional formatting", but this is just a sub-task in the larger task of getting formatting to work in Excel. Simply solving the sub-task causes frustration and annoyance if you can't also solve the larger task.

A small number of search terms represent a very substantial quantity of search behavior—a search Long Neck. This Long Neck has been around for quite a while. In 2002, Richard Wiggins, a senior information technologist at Michigan State University, found that the top 1,000 searches represented 50% of search behavior on their site. In fact, the "top 30 search phrases represent some 15% of the 200,000 searches performed over a period of several weeks," Wiggins wrote.

The following table shows Long Neck behavior on a large intranet.

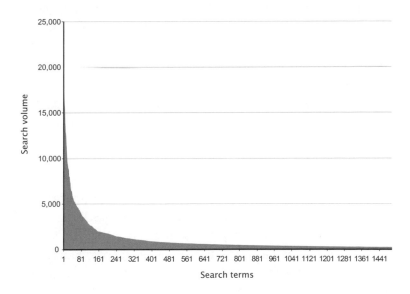

Of the 1,500 top searches over a six-month period, 5% (or 75 search terms) represent 35% of search volume.

Hitwise is an online market research company. In 2008, Bill Tancer, its general manager for global research, published the following set of data:

- **Top 100 terms: 5.7% of all search traffic**
- **Top 500 terms: 8.9% of all search traffic**
- **Top 1,000 terms: 10.6% of all search traffic**
- **Top 10,000 terms: 18.5% of all search traffic**

He pointed out that "This means if you had a monopoly over the top 1,000 search terms across all search engines (which is impossible), you'd still be missing out on 89.4% of all search traffic. There's so much traffic in the tail it is hard to even comprehend."

So, 100 search terms got only 5.7% of all search traffic. That's not much, is it? How about we put it this way: Tancer had analyzed 14 million search terms. So, out of 14 million search terms analyzed, 100 got 5.7% of search traffic. That means that 0.000007% of search terms got 5.7% of all search traffic. 10,000 terms (or 0.07%) out of 14 million got 18.5% of all search traffic.

The tail is very exciting—on the surface. It's a bit like saying that we're only using a tiny fraction of matter in the universe. True. But what is the cost of making the rest of this matter usable? I'm not saying ignore the tail. What I am saying is absolutely do not ignore the neck. Given scarce resources there is far more to be gained by making sure that all of your Long Neck search terms are easy to find.

Also remember that "IMSUM function" exists in the tail and "sum numbers" exists in the neck. If we optimize "IMSUM function" for the few we risk confusing the "sum numbers" search for the many. Every action has a reaction. By making search easier for one page, we potentially make it more difficult for another. We must make sure that we are not doing stuff down in the tail that is disrupting activity in the neck. That would be truly counterproductive.

The patterns and rules of search are out there. They just need to be observed and acted on.

STUDENTS' LONG NECK SEARCH

What do students really want from a university Web site? According to a 2008 study of the UK Open University Web site, the top tasks were:

1. Can I study (my subject)?

2. What does it cost?

3. What qualification will I earn, and how will this help me in my job or career?

4. Where do I go to take this course?

5. Can I study part time, while working?

These top tasks map extremely well to the top task identification studies we have performed over a number of years. When the presenters analyzed search behavior on the Open University Web site, they found that the search terms used mapped well to the top tasks. The research also found that:

- a small number of terms are extremely popular (Long Neck);
- there is a very large number of infrequently used terms (Long Tail);
- even in the tail, the themes of the top search terms persist.

The study found that there is often a strong relationship between the Long Neck search terms and Long Tail search terms. Have a look at the following table which lists a sample of searches connected with classical studies.

Search Term	Search Volume
classical studies	81
classical studies department	12
classical latin	8
classical greek	7
classics courses	7
classics department	6
classical studies diploma	5
classical studies dept	3
classical studies Web site	3
classical studies webpage	2
classical greece	1
classical texts	1

"Classical studies" had 81 searches and is well out in front—it's in the Long Neck. "Classical studies Web site" (three searches) and "classical studies webpage" (two searches) are in the Long Tail. Based on our prior knowledge that the top task is "subject/ course", let's say we focus on making sure that when someone searches for "classical studies" the first result is a link to classical studies courses, with the second link perhaps being to the classical studies department homepage. If we work to optimize the search so that the first result will be the courses link then we will help the Long Tail searches such as "classical studies Web site" and "classical studies webpage".

Of course, there is much more to do here. Classical and classics are clearly related. If someone searches for "classical Greece", then we should deliver a search result for "classical Greek courses". You see, this is not technology, it's psychology.

PRESIDENT BARACK OBAMA'S LONG NECK

The patterns and rules are out there, they just need observing. In August 2008 I analyzed search terms connected with Barack Obama and John McCain. Here's what I found:

- **The top search term for Barack Obama was "barack obama". Out of 150 related search terms with 2,424,080 searches it had 1,830,000, representing 75% of overall search volume.**
- **The top search term for John McCain was "john mccain". Out of 150 related search terms with 888,797 searches it had 673,000, representing 76% of overall search volume.**
- **If you took out the term "barack obama" and analyzed the other 149 related searches, then the top 5% got 29% of the remaining vote.**
- **If you took out the term "john mccain" and analyzed the other 149 related searches, then the top 5% got 28% of the remaining vote.**
- **The top seven search terms from the remaining 149 for Barack Obama got as much of the vote as the bottom 106.**
- **The top seven search terms from the remaining 149 for John McCain got as much of the vote as the bottom 108.**

This shows an obvious pattern. There are always patterns and rules. A good manager identifies the underlying patterns and rules so that he can make appropriate decisions based on them.

You don't manage people's ability to search on your Web site. You manage their ability to find on your Web site.

TOP SEARCH WORDS ARE NOT ALWAYS THE SAME AS TOP TASKS

People often say to me: "We already know our top tasks. Even if we don't, all we have to do is look at the top searches or the most visited pages."

If only it were that simple. Search is a window into what is important to people, but there are many other windows in people's minds. Knowing the words people search for is just one of them. I once worked with a large organization whose intranet had lots and lots of search for factory and office locations.

When we did a bit of research we found that nobody owned the "Find a Location" task and because of this each division tended to create maps and location details for themselves. There's an interesting point here. The location data that was being created was not for the division that created it but rather for the most popular locations that employees from that division needed to visit.

The result was that there was a proliferation of location information on the intranet. There were often multiple maps of the same location, some of them useful, some of them badly drawn and/or totally out of date. It was a mess.

The organization decided to do something about it. They cleaned out all the old location data and created a central "Find a Location" resource that was easy to find through the navigation, well designed, and kept up to date. Over a 12-month period, search for location-type words significantly declined. Does that mean "Find a Location" became a less important task? No. It just means that people didn't need to use the search engine as much to find a location.

Another organization we worked with used to take the top 10 search words and publish them on their homepage under a "Quick Links" heading. ("Quick Links" is such a strange name. Are the other links "Slow Links?" I would strongly advise against using "Quick Links" as a heading for any group of links. It is a nonsensical term.

Do you know what happened? Search for these words declined because links to them were now easily available on the homepage. So, after a couple of months, there was a new set of top 10 search words. This new top 10 became the new "Quick Links". Can you guess what happened then? People started complaining about the old "Quick Links" being removed. They were being searched for again and soon became the new top 10.

There is a particular problem with depending too much on top search results data from the organization's own search engine. Usually, this search engine is so bad that people only use it as a last resort, so looking at its search data doesn't really give you the full picture.

Nor does looking at the most visited pages on your Web site. The most popular page is usually the homepage but what does that tell you? Or let's say it's the support homepage. But the support homepage has loads of tasks on it. Which ones are the top tasks? In fact, many pages have a range of top tasks on them.

What about the top tasks customers couldn't complete because the right page was badly named or badly organized and thus unfindable? And what about pages that are popular for all the wrong reasons—for example because their name misleads the customers into thinking that they are about one thing when in fact they are about something very different? (For example, people searching with "sum a number" on the Microsoft Excel Web site and finding IMSUM function content.)

And what happens when the words people search for are not the words they want to read when they arrive at a page? Millions of people search for "cheap hotels". Does that mean they want to read "Welcome to our dirt cheap hotel" when they arrive at the webpage? So, search is extremely important, but it doesn't always tell you the whole story.

A METHOD FOR MANAGING SEARCH

Nobody wants to search. Given the option would you prefer to have your car key sitting on the desk in front of you or would you prefer to go searching for it? We don't like Google because it's a search engine, we like it because it's a find engine. So, you don't manage people's ability to search on your Web site. You manage their ability to find on your Web site.

This is a method which will help you accurately measure how easy it is to find the most searched-for content on your Web site. It involves the following steps:

1. Identify approximately the top 400 search words/phrases on your Web site.

2. Identify the correct search result for each of these search terms.

3. Search for each of these top search terms using your search engine and the Google public search engine.

4. Based on our formula, which I'll explain later, a search success rate is calculated.

Identify the top search words/phrases

Identify the search terms that make up 25–50% of search volume on your Web site over a 12-month period. For larger Web sites we're talking about somewhere between 200 and 1,000 search terms. It's better to choose a 12-month period because this will allow for seasonal variations.

Identify the correct page for each of the search words

Now that you have identified the most-searched-for terms, identify the correct page for each of them. So, if "training" is a top search term, then the best page would be the "Training" homepage. In some situations, there may be more than one correct page.

You will need to work with various experts throughout your organization to identify the correct pages, as it's not a simple job. Remember the example of "Remove conditional formatting"? The correct page is not always as obvious as it seems. Take your time and get it right.

The first step in improving findability is taking each search word whose correct page is not the first result and fixing the reason why.

Search with the top search words

According to analysis of millions of searches carried out on the America Online Web site, 64% of people will click within the first three search results and 90% will click within the first 10. Basically, more people have been on top of Mount Everest than have been to the 15th page of search results. (Does it even exist?) Parents today warn their children: "Johnny, don't go beyond the fifth page of search results." I have seen the same basic pattern in other research into where people click on a search results page.

Go to your search engine and search with each of the top search words. Use the following table—compiled from the America Online research—to allocate scores based on the correct page's position in the search results.

Search Result	Score
1st	42
2nd	12
3rd	8
4th	6
5th	5

Search Result	Score
6th	4
7th	4
8th	3
9th	3
10th	3
11th and so on	0

For example:

1. **If the correct page is first, give that particular search term 42;**

2. **If it is fourth give it six;**

3. **If it is outside the top 10, give it 0.**

So, if the search term was "classical studies" and the first result was the classical studies courses page, then you would allocate a score of 42 for that particular search. If the classical studies courses link was second, it would get a score of 12.

In a test with 400 search words a 100% score would be 16,800 (400 x 42 = 16,800). In other words, for each of the 400 search words the correct page came first in the search results every time.

Remember that you should always judge based on the organic or actual search results. In other words, the 10 search results on the search results page. Anything else (Did You Mean, Best Bets, Manual Recommendations, Key Matches) does not count for this particular measure.

The reason is that these techniques are quick fixes. They do not solve the underlying problem with the search engine. By focusing on improving the organic search results for the top search terms, you will improve the search results for many other searches.

IMPROVING THE SUCCESS RATE

Your job is now to increase the search success-rate figure. Day by day, search result by search result, you will make it better. Remember, making search work is never a launch-and-leave project but rather a process of continuous improvement. Web sites evolve as new content is added and old content is removed. So, while the "Training" homepage might be first today when someone searches for "training", it could have slipped in the ranking when you check again in six months.

The first step in improving findability is to go through each search word whose correct page is not the first result and fix the reason why. To start this process, get the first search word whose correct page didn't make first place and search with it.

Identify where exactly the correct page ranks in the search results. Is it fourth or 44th? Wherever it is, your job is to get it to first place, or as close to first place as possible.

Use the following checklist when examining the first page of search results for the top search words.

1. **Are these search results relevant** to what has been searched for? If the word "training" was searched for, are the results at least in some way related to training? If not, why not?

2. **Are the results very minor pages** and/or pages that most customers will never need to find? Then consider removing them from the search indexing process or at least de-emphasizing them by, for example, removing key search terms from their title tags and page content.

3. **Do the search results reflect logical, alternative** versions of the search term? (If people search for "planet" on the BBC Web site they will get lots of search results for outer space and the solar system. But they may also get some results for a program called *The Blue Planet*, which is about the sea.)

4. **Is there a good variety** of search results, rather than most of them linking to the same basic place?

5. **Are there duplicate search results?** If so, you need to remove them from the search results, and may even need to delete them entirely. Remember, not every search result that looks like a duplicate is a duplicate. Sometimes it's because of duplicate metadata, while the actual pages may be different. This is one reason why it's important to click each search result that you're testing.

6. **Does the text of each result contain the words** being searched for? People are confused by search results that do not contain the words they searched for. So, if "training" was searched for, then the search result should contain the word "training", or at the very least a relevant synonym.

7. **Does the text of each result logically describe the page** it is linking to? Perhaps because of some mistake by whoever wrote the text for the search results, it contains the word "training" but the page it links to is either not about training or is only vaguely related to training.

8. **Does each search result work?** Or do some of them link to pages that no longer exist? This could indicate an indexing problem with the search engine.

9. **Is the search result restricted somehow?** Does it require
    a log-in of some sort? In such situations, if the person
    doing the searching has not been logged-in—or perhaps
    is not authorized to see this page—they should not see
    links that will lead them to access-restricted or other
    error-type messages. Instead, send them to an available
    page that explains various access restrictions and/or has
    a log-in option.

Always try to understand the underlying reasons for poor-quality
search results. For example, if in an intranet search for "training"
you are getting back employee details, then that could indicate
that the employee directory is mixed in with the general search
results. Try to get to the root of the issue because fixing the root
problem will have a huge impact on findability. And always
remember: Search management is more about psychology than
technology.

chapter 12

Deliver what customers want—not what you want

Your body plays tricks on your mind. You cannot be trusted.

Ben Goldacre

WHAT YOU ARE AND WHAT YOU WANT TO BE

One of the most common conversations I've had with managers over the years is about the challenge of balancing where their organizations are now with where they want to be. Many organizations have a "bread and butter" function—something basic that they are very good at. That's why they are successful and why customers come to them. Maybe this function won't be important to where they need to be in five years' time, but it's very important today and the top task as of right now. As such, managers face a dilemma: Adding new stuff will make this task more difficult to complete.

And other factors are at play in the challenge to balance present with future. Boredom is one of them. People get bored doing something they have become very good at. Sometimes this successful thing was built by a previous group of managers. The current group wants to make their mark, too, by building a successful service or product.

Sometimes the top task is not as profitable. There is other stuff that is much more cost effective to sell, and if that stuff was pushed more, more people would buy it. And then there is the world of organization silos. The web team may not have control over the top task. They may be a part of to another department or division, perhaps part of the communications or marketing departments whereas the top task is "owned" by the IT department.

There are many reasons why customers' top tasks do not get top priority from organizations. However, the harsh reality is that, given a choice, web customers will leave your site if you do not allow them to complete their top tasks quickly and easily. If they have to complete the task with you they will pick up the phone or walk into an office. They will be frustrated and annoyed because one of the greatest sins in this modern age is wasting your customers' time.

WHAT MICROSOFT WANTS

Microsoft wants to sell lots of software and make lots of money. It's a very normal company that has had abnormal success. And just like every other organization on the planet, what Microsoft wants is not always what the customer wants.

Microsoft Pinpoint is a Web site that helps business customers find IT solutions built on Microsoft technologies and helps Microsoft partners market their offerings. In particular, it focuses on helping small and medium businesses find qualified experts, software applications, and professional services that address their unique issues. You'd go to Pinpoint if you needed outside IT expertise and wanted a solution based on Microsoft technologies.

Microsoft wanted to identify the technology-related top tasks that made small and medium businesses seek outside help, so that they could better understand and address customer needs. What kind of task would bring them to a Web site like Microsoft Pinpoint?

At a certain level you'd think that there can't be top tasks here. This is so broad: We're talking about the whole world of IT; all the software and technology that small and medium businesses use to address a vast array of challenges.

Here's a sample of the type of tasks we came up with after exhaustive research:

1. Accounting (general ledger, accounts receivable/payable, job costing, order entry)

2. Antivirus (software, consultancy, malware)

3. Backup and recovery (online, archiving)

4. Customer relationship management (CRM, Microsoft Dynamics, customer care/satisfaction)

5. Data migration/integration

6. Desktop support

7. Financial analytics and reporting

8. Hosting (Web, ecommerce, E-mail, co-location, SharePoint, Exchange)

9. Internet security

10. Network design (LAN, WAN, wireless, VPNs, VoIP)

11. Order management

12. Payroll (services, time, and attendance tracking)

13. Spam (anti-spam, filters, blockers, blacklists)

14. Supply chain management

15. Tax management

It's quite a broad sample isn't it? We asked about 700 small and medium businesses throughout the United States to score their top tasks. (The core focus was organizations with between five and 250 PCs.) These organizations worked in many different sectors, including technology, government, healthcare, manufacturing, retail, and hospitality. Another broad range. Here's a list of the top tasks that we identified:

Tasks	Total Vote	% of Total Vote 7395	Cumulative Vote	Cumulative Carewords
Internet security	236	3%	3%	1%
Antivirus (software, consultancy, malware)	222	3%	6%	2%
Computer/PC support (maintenance, repair, slow computer, performance)	204	3%	9%	3%
Backup and recovery (online, archiving)	194	3%	12%	4%
E-mail management (software, services, hosting, security)	179	2%	14%	5%
Security (audits, intrusion detection, prevention, updates)	171	2%	16%	6%
Spyware (blockers, removal)	167	2%	19%	7%
Desktop support	165	2%	21%	8%
Desktop/office software	140	2%	23%	9%
Training (IT, computer, Web-based)	136	2%	25%	10%
Servers (hosting, monitoring, data, dedicated)	128	2%	26%	11%
Data/document management	124	2%	28%	12%
Customer service (development, fulfillment, call tracking)	120	2%	30%	13%
Database (design, management, administration, support)	119	2%	31%	14%
Spam (anti-spam, filters, blockers, blacklists)	118	2%	33%	15%
Payroll (services, time, and attendance tracking)	117	2%	34%	16%
Secure data communication	117	2%	36%	18%
Employee Internet use, monitoring, filtering	116	2%	37%	19%
Network and wireless security	114	2%	39%	20%
Storage (devices, online, archive)	114	2%	41%	21%

You could look at the preceding list and say that's not a very Long Neck because the top 5% of tasks only got 14% of the vote. And that's a good point. My counter-argument is that we were probably too refined in our choice of tasks. Internet security, Antivirus, Security, and Spyware are all strongly related and if we add them together we get 10% overall. Computer/PC support and Desktop support are also quite closely related and together they add up to 5%.

An interesting point is the stability of the results, which can be seen in the following table. What it shows is that the top tasks had emerged by the first quarter of the vote (179 voters), and that there was very little change as the voting progressed.

Tasks	179 Voters	358 Voters	537 Voters	716 Voters
Internet security	3%	3%	3%	3%
Antivirus (software, consultancy, malware)	2%	2%	3%	3%
Computer/PC support (maintenance, repair, slow computer, performance)	3%	3%	3%	3%
Backup and recovery (online, archiving)	3%	3%	3%	3%
E-mail management (software, services, hosting, security)	2%	2%	2%	2%
Security (audits, intrusion detection, prevention, updates)	3%	2%	2%	2%
Spyware (blockers, removal)	3%	2%	2%	2%
Desktop support	3%	3%	2%	2%
Desktop/office software	2%	2%	2%	2%
Training (IT, computer, Web-based)	2%	2%	2%	2%
Servers (hosting, monitoring, data, dedicated)	1%	1%	2%	2%
Data/document management	2%	1%	2%	2%

There is a clear message from the results. Security is the top task, which makes sense when you think about it. A security issue is a trigger issue—it's what sends you on that search or makes you pick up the phone—and it's something you can't resolve yourself. Internet security is particularly important and this is true regardless of the number of PCs an organization has, or whether an organization has fewer than 10 employees or more than 500.

We asked the Microsoft team responsible for the Pinpoint Web site to vote on the tasks while trying to think like their customers. Then we compared the two votes. The following table shows the tasks that were statistically most important to each group:

Customer	Microsoft
Internet security	Customer relationship management
Backup and recovery	Internet marketing
Security	Network management
Desktop support	Sales/lead generation
Data/document management	Billing

While Internet security was a top task for customers, it didn't rate highly for the Microsoft team. On the other hand, while customer relationship management was the top task for the Microsoft team, it didn't rate highly for customers.

Security is something that has become more and more important to Microsoft's customers. Yet, when the Pinpoint team was presented with the results of the vote, they were indeed surprised. They hadn't downplayed security deliberately; they just hadn't considered it a top task. They had a vision of small and medium business that was more about Internet marketing than Internet security. As a result, Microsoft has gradually shifted its focus and made security solutions more central among its offers.

The original version of the Pinpoint homepage also came from a classic marketing perspective.

The hero shot dominated the page, with the implication that this handsome man (with his arms folded) uses Pinpoint, and you should too. The new version of the page that came out of the top task identification project was much more to the point.

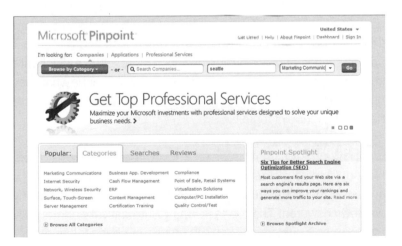

On the new page, "Search" is much more obvious, with an added location option as businesses often require technical help that is located nearby. Categories now feature on the homepage, with the top tasks of "Internet security" and "Computer/PC management" being quite prominent. These simple but powerful changes reflect the philosophy that top tasks should be prominent and doable. A great webpage is not something to look at. It's something to do practical things on it.

"This philosophy is now integrated into everything we do and we have continued to refine our site with key customer tasks in mind," states Peter Horsman, global site management lead for Microsoft Pinpoint. "Most users now enter Pinpoint through a search results page tailored specifically to what they are looking for. This helps our customers find what they need quickly, while allowing them the option of refining the search outcome further."

"Our work with Gerry increased understanding across our team of the specific tasks that our customers are trying to accomplish and how best to address their needs," Peter continues. "We adopted the mantra that customers use the site to get something done—in our case, finding a Microsoft technology expert, and contacting that company about its application or service. From this standpoint, we identified browse categories and refined our use of images and our overall design. The result is a significant improvement (+20%) in our customers' ability to find what they need on Pinpoint. The study is now standard reading for anyone new to the Pinpoint team."

THE SUPER TASK

How do people make the decision to buy a car navigation/GPS system? That's the question a consumer electronics company wanted answered. The top task was: "Automatically and quickly recalculates a new route if you miss a turn or change your plans". It got a massive 12% of the vote. However, when we asked a number of company product managers to vote, there was no overlap between the customers' top 10 tasks and the top 10 tasks of the organization. There was a major disconnect, as can be seen from the following table, which details the top 10 tasks for each group.

Customer	Organization
Automatically and quickly recalculates a new route if you miss a turn or change your plans	Perfect integration into the dashboard
3D moving maps to help you navigate more easily	Best brand in navigation
Easy-to-follow, accurate directions	Industry-leading pinpoint accuracy even when GPS signal lets you down (tunnel, high rises, forest, etc.)
Full postcode searches	Internet and Web access
Bright and clear anti-glare screen	Really easy to use even by people not familiar with the technology
Clear friendly spoken instructions	Free live traffic information: Great way to avoid traffic problems
Drive safely: Voice control allows you to keep your eyes on the road	Free professional fitting
Easy update software and maps	Navigate 26 countries—straight out the box
Bluetooth-enabled (phone and music)	State-of-the-art GPS, music centre and Bluetooth all in one unit
Most up-to-date map information	Plays CDs and DVDs in almost every possible format (MP3, AAC, WMA, DIVX)

In this particular example, not one of the top tasks overlaps. It is a classic case of the organization seeing the world in one way and the customer seeing it in another.

Have a look at the customers' top task again:

Automatically and quickly recalculates a new route if you miss a turn or change your plans.

Out of 93 tasks it got a whopping 12% of the vote. People made this their top vote whether they were thinking of buying for business or personal use, whether they were under 25 or over 45, whether or not they were a customer of this particular company, whether they already owned a navigation system or were planning to buy their first one.

This is what I've come to call the **super task**. It's way out in front of everything else. For example, the next most popular task, "3D moving maps to help you navigate more easily", had 7% of the vote, a whole 5% less than the top task.

"Find people" is often by far the super task on large intranets. "Find a course/subject" is usually the super task for a university, as is "Book a room" for a hotel, and "Book a flight" for an airline. Do you have a super task? If you do, you should give it overwhelming prominence on your Web site. At a minimum, it must be dominating and doable on your homepage.

chapter 13

Measuring success: Back to basics

We see the struggle of intuition, personal experience, and philosophical inclination waging war against the brute force of numbers.

Ian Ayres

THE CULT OF VOLUME

The number of pages that customers visit is probably the worst possible measure of success for a Web site. If Customer A visits 20 pages on your Web site and Customer B visits 10, what does that mean? Customer A could be confused by the navigation and search and might be very frustrated at the end of those 20 pages. Alternatively, they might leave the site satisfied because they found exactly what they wanted. We simply don't know which customer had the better experience.

Customer A spends two minutes on a Web site while Customer B spends four. Which is better? All things being equal, two minutes is better than four. It's less time, and the number one thing you should manage is your customers' time. But what if Customer B completed their task and Customer A didn't? It's all about the context of the task.

In 2005, User Interface Engineering conducted a study on a number of retail ecommerce Web sites. In the study, the ideal Web site would transact $1,000 of merchandise. Gap was the best performer with $660. Macy's did not do too well with $156, and Newport News was at the bottom with $63.

Sales per thousand dollars

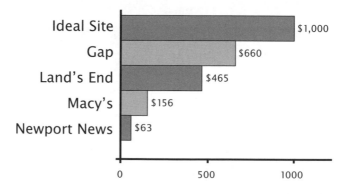

User Interface Engineering (UIE.COM), 2005

When they did extra analysis to see why Gap was doing so much better than Macy's or Newport News, they collected the following data on the number of pages customers were visiting.

Number of pages to purchase

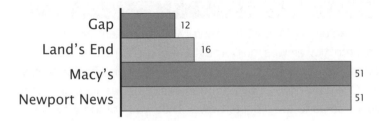

Gap	12
Land's End	16
Macy's	51
Newport News	51

User Interface Engineering (UIE.COM), 2005

The average number of pages a typical customer visited on Gap's Web site before they purchased was 12. The average number for Macy's or Newport News was 51. Only a very dedicated customer would visit 51 pages in order to buy a pair of jeans. This all makes perfect sense when you think like a customer trying to buy a pair of jeans. The more pages, the more time, the more frustration. Of course, you need to visit a certain number of pages in order to see the range and make your choice, but not 51.

TIME AND MOTION REVISITED

Frederick Taylor is regarded by many as the father of management. Author and management consultant Peter Drucker described Taylor's work as "The most powerful as well as the most lasting contribution America has made to Western thought since the Federalist Papers."

Frederick Taylor was a usability geek. He spent much of his professional life watching how people shoveled coal or cut steel. Taylor believed that things could be broken down and understood through careful observation and analysis. It's time to take Taylor's ideas and apply them to the information factories. Today, these information factories are as inefficient and unproductive as the physical factories Taylor found in the latter half of the 19th century. This is a huge opportunity for you; to be part of a revolution in how we complete tasks by using content.

A PROBLEM WITH BELTS

In the factories of the 1890s there was a problem with belts. At that time power was delivered through a "forest of belts", as Robert Kanigel writes in his book about Frederick Taylor entitled *The One Best Way*. The common wisdom was to make belts thinner so as to keep costs down. That was not the way Taylor thought. He wanted to make them thicker.

Taylor, you see, was addressing a different issue, as fellow engineer William Kent pointed out. "Taylor was actually tackling a new problem," wrote Kent. It wasn't about how wide and thick a belt must be to transmit a certain amount of horsepower but, rather, to transmit it "with the minimum cost for belt repairs, the longest life to the belt, and the smallest loss and inconvenience from stopping the machine while the belt is being tightened or repaired…To him, they weren't so much transmitters of power as potential impediments to production…When the belts broke, the machines stopped, and the factory grew still. And this must not be."

Many organizations view Web site content in the same way belts were viewed back in those belt-breaking days: They want it cheap and thin. Today, Taylor would not be concerned so much with the content itself as its impact on the production process. Is this content helping or hindering productivity? This is a giant opportunity to use content to drive efficiency and productivity.

IT'S WHAT YOU DO WITH THE TIME

Simonds Rolling Machine Company of Massachusetts made steel balls. In 1896, the demand for such balls was high and growing.

However, there was a bottleneck in the production process: Quality control.

"To the untrained eye, the dazzling steel spheres came from the long row of grinding and polishing machines looking alike and looking perfect," wrote Robert Kanigel. "But much could go wrong. Fire cracks from heat treating, soft spots, rough spots, flat spots—sometimes due to faulty steel, sometimes to the machines."

By focusing on the inspection method, Taylor reduced the working day from 10 and a half hours to eight and a half. Within months, 35 women were doing the work that 120 had done before and were making almost double their original wages.

Frederick Taylor was focused on making every minute productive; on working smart rather than working hard. He would be shocked at the sheer crudeness of the way most Web sites are managed today. It's time for a revolution in Web site management.

THREE METRICS OF TASK SUCCESS

Over the years, I have developed a method for measuring task success. I call it the Task Performance Indicator (TPI). The three key metrics of the TPI are:

1. Success rate

2. Disaster rate

3. Completion time

The Task Performance Indicator was developed with input from Rolf Molich. Rolf is a brilliant usability expert from Denmark who has spent much of his professional life observing and learning from people as they seek to use software or Web sites.

Success rate

If your customers can't complete the top tasks they came to your Web site to complete, your Web site fails. This is the essential base measure. The essence of understanding the success rate is understanding the task. For years, ecommerce Web sites were concerned about their very high shopping-cart abandon rates. They assumed that everyone who entered the shopping-cart process had an initial intent to buy.

Many people who add stuff to a shopping cart are interested in the total cost of the product (including shipping). They are concerned about the hidden extras that often get added to a product's price. So, if that was their task and they got the answer, then their task was completed. Before you know if a task was successfully completed or not, you need to know what it was.

Disaster rate

A disaster occurs when a customer thinks they have completed the task but have in fact gotten the wrong answer. A disaster is a very serious situation with potential legal implications. We have found that the disaster rate is the most powerful metric to use when trying to get the attention of senior management.

How can a disaster occur? Employees were asked to use the intranet of Organization A to find out what percentage of the organization's customers was dissatisfied according to the most recent customer satisfaction survey. A number of people searched for "Customer satisfaction survey". When they saw that the first result contained the text "customer satisfaction survey" they immediately clicked it. This result stated that 24% of customers were dissatisfied. The correct answer was actually 14%. How did that happen? The first result was for an out-of-date version of the survey.

Old content affects new content. The older the Web site, the greater the proportion of old content to new content. Let's say an organization has been running customer satisfaction surveys for

10 years. There are thus nine years of archived surveys and one current survey. Every year the survey archive grows bigger but there is still only one current survey.

Completion time

If the success rate and disaster rate are "fixing the basics", then the completion time is best practice. On an intersection in New York there are five Starbucks: Four on each corner, and one about 15 feet away from one of the corners. Most of the time, they're not very full.

Starbucks isn't just in the business of making coffee, it's also in the business of self-service, which means it must manage the customer's time. There are lots of offices around this intersection and there are rush times during the day. Starbucks knows that if the queue is too long, people stop joining it.

By far the most important thing you can manage on your Web site is your customers' time. If you really want a world class public Web site or intranet you must become absolutely and utterly obsessed with saving your customers' time. There is nothing more important. Nothing.

The Scottish McDonald brothers were obsessed with time. Their breakthrough in San Bernardino of the 1950s was to create a Taylor-like production line for the production of burgers—not too many ingredients, consistently produced, and at a great price. News spread about how fast and cheap it was to eat at McDonald's, and the rest, as they say, is history.

Starbucks is fast coffee. McDonald's is fast food. The Web is fast tasks.

"Optimal time" is also something we need to compute. This is essentially the time it should take to complete the task under optimal conditions. We need to know how the completion time for a particular task compares with its optimal time. Is the task completion time already optimal? Is it twice as slow as it should be? Is it three times, four times?

Calculating the optimal time is not essential to getting task measurement going, but calculating the success rate is a great start. If you can show that 40% of customers who try to complete top tasks give up, that is a strong and compelling message. Showing that 10% of them get the wrong answer even though they think it's correct should get management to pay attention. Improving the success rate and reducing the disaster rate is an excellent start.

Organizations don't care how long it takes their employees or customers to complete tasks.

PRESENTING INDIVIDUAL TASK MEASUREMENT RESULTS

The following is an example of how we present results. The project was for the OECD.

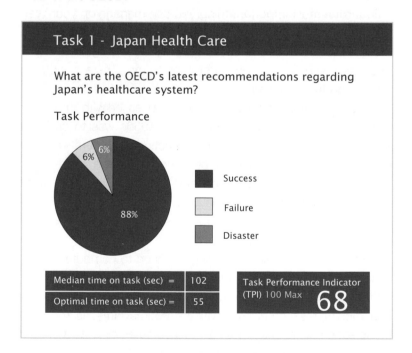

The Task Performance Indicator (TPI) score for this example is 68. The TPI is a somewhat complicated formula that takes the following into account:

1. **Success rate:** The higher the success rate, the higher the TPI will be.

2. **Failure rate:** The lower the failure rate, the higher the TPI will be.

3. **Disaster rate:** This is treated differently from a normal failure. A large disaster rate will have a significant impact on the TPI.

4. **Completion time:** A type of sliding scale is used to compute the impact of time. At a very basic level, the longer the time taken beyond the optimal time, the lower the TPI.

WHY ORGANIZATIONS DON'T CARE ABOUT PRODUCTIVITY

Organizations are strange when it comes to managing time in relation to content-based tasks. Basically, they don't care how long it takes their employees or customers to complete tasks. It's not relevant, and not important from a management perspective. One reason is that it's hard to accurately measure how much time is being wasted. (The fact that it's hard does not mean it should not be done.) Part of it is down to the fact that managers are not trained to manage content-based tasks.

I once told a manager that it was really difficult for employees to find an office/factory location using the intranet. There were lots of duplicate and out-of-date maps of the same cities and locations. Nobody was in charge and nobody cared. I told the manager that with a bit of management the organization could save five minutes every time an employee looked for a location. The manager looked at me and shrugged. "They could be out smoking a cigarette," was his reply.

Here's the paradox. Managers and other employees are always saying that they're very busy, that they don't have enough time. You offer them a way to have more time and they're not interested. Why is that? At one level, time seems to be one of the most valuable resources an organization has. At another it's irrelevant and trivial and can be wasted at will. Who cares how long it takes to find people, book meeting rooms, find product images, or find and understand a procedure or policy?

As the task becomes more complex and less frequent, it makes sense to move it to the phone or to face-to-face support.

A PRODUCTIVE CALL TO ARMS

This is a call to arms: We are now on the verge of a revolution in management. It will focus on the management of content-based tasks. The Web will be the crucible of this revolution; time will be the spear point.

If ever a manager dismisses the fact that you are saving time, and says that in that five minutes you have just saved, employees could be out smoking a cigarette, here's your answer:

"Yes, they could be. But how they use those five minutes is your responsibility. It is management's job to make sure time is used in the most productive manner possible. Right now, those five minutes are lost to the organization. It's wasted time; gone. By making the Web site task more efficient, the five minutes become available again. If that task is done a hundred times a day, the time saved is equivalent to having an extra employee."

Productivity on the Web is based on the principle of self-service.

- The best self-service tasks have high frequency and low complexity
- The worst self-service tasks have low frequency and high complexity

The Web is not good for everything. As the task becomes more complex and less frequent, it makes sense to move it to the phone or to face-to-face support. If you force a task that is more optimally completed by phone on to the Web, then all you do is frustrate your customers and waste their time and money—as well as yours.

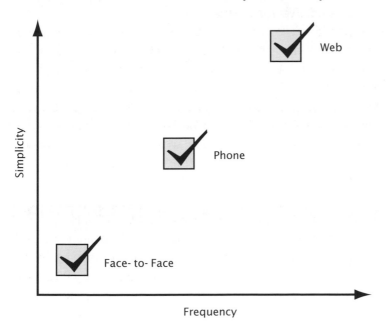

When deciding whether or not a task should be completed on the Web, keep two key issues in mind:

1. **The complexity of the task: The more complex it is, the less likely it is that the customer will want to—or be able to—complete it online.**

2. **The frequency or demand: The less frequent the demand for the task, the less likely it is to show a return on investment.**

Isn't it great to be able to go online and choose your own seat on a plane? Remember how in the past the airline attendant just handed you a ticket, or at best asked you if you wanted an aisle or window seat? Now you can do it well in advance and the chances of getting the exact seat you want increase. This is self-service at work. It saves money for the airline and makes you more empowered. Everybody wins.

Suppose your local hospital said to you: "We're introducing self-service for X-ray analysis. You interpret the results yourself. It's cheaper and you will feel more empowered." Would you be jumping for joy? The more complex the task, the less suited it is for self-service. Management is about understanding the lines of complexity. It's about knowing when a task is so complex that it requires face-to-face support and when a task is simple enough that it can work on the Web. The Web does not solve every problem.

THE TRUE COST OF A SELF-SERVICE TASK

According to research in 2009, it cost a UK local authority £9.34 to help a customer complete a task in a face-to-face situation. It cost £3.76 for the same task over the phone, but only £0.27 if the task was completed on the Web. That's a compelling business case isn't it? £0.27 versus £9.34, well, that's an easy choice. Let's put everything on the Web and we'll all be superstars.

Except that it's not quite that simple. The £0.27 we are talking about is the variable, or per-transaction, cost. The fixed cost is missing. How much does it cost to build and maintain the Web site, to write and test the content, to design and test the forms and applications? That's the fixed cost and, in a self-service world, fixed costs can be quite high. (That's why McDonald's won't set up in a small village.) Face-to-face fixed costs, on the other hand, tend to be low. You've got two people—the customer and the employee—interacting.

	Fixed Cost	Variable Cost
Web	£40,000	£0.27
Phone	£15,000	£3.76
Face-to-Face	£5,000	£9.34

Let's say that a particular company's fixed costs are: £40,000 for its Web site, £15,000 for phone support, and £5,000 for face-to-face support. What does that mean?

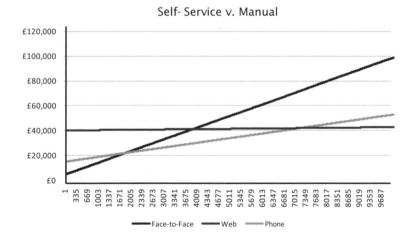

It means that up until about 1,600 transactions it would actually be cheaper to take the face-to-face option; that the phone would be cheaper up to about 4,000 transactions, and only after that would the Web site show a return on investment. So, not only is the Web not always the best option for certain tasks from a customer's point of view, for some tasks it is also not the most cost-effective one.

Self-service only works if it works

What happens if someone goes to a Web site to complete a task and fails? You either lose them as a customer or they will ring you, E-mail you, or walk into your office. The cost of failure for self-service has two parts:

1. The cost of the failed self-service task.

2. The cost of the manual service interaction.

A badly managed Web site will thus add overheads and cost to the organization. It will be the opposite of a magic solution. Local authorities should put everything on the Web because it only costs £0.27 per task completion, whereas a face-to-face task completion costs £9.34. Of course, that logic only works if the Web site works and, according to a 2009 survey for GovMetric, customers are not very happy with local authority Web sites.

While 67% of respondents were happy with face-to-face interactions and 89% were happy with phone interactions, only 49% were happy with Web site interactions. The number one reason for dissatisfaction was "query not resolved". In other words, task not completed. Think of it this way: The customer fails to complete the task online. That costs £0.27. They ring up. That costs £3.76. What's the total cost? It's £0.27 plus £3.76, which equals £4.03. The Web site that is supposed to be saving money is actually costing money. The Web site only works when customers can complete tasks.

chapter 14

Preparing for task measurement

We know less than we think we do about our own minds, and exert less control over our own minds than we think…This schism between what people do and what they say persists into adulthood.

Timothy D. Wilson

REAL PEOPLE, TOP TASKS

I once gave a talk to a group of computer programmers. I was trying to convince them that watching real people try to use the Web sites and applications they were responsible for was a good thing. They were skeptical, to say the least. One statement summed up the feeling in the room:

I don't want to waste my time watching people.

That room was full of smart people who felt that they had more important things to do than watch their customers. Ray Kroc, who built McDonald's, would not have agreed. Sam Walton, who built Wal-Mart, would not have agreed. These titans of self-service spent their lives keenly observing the human species.

When Ray Kroc heard about the McDonald brothers' restaurant, he was intrigued. He headed out to San Bernardino and for two days sat in his car on a hill overlooking the building. He observed the restaurant from the moment the first worker arrived early in the morning until the moment it closed for the day. On the afternoon of the second day, he walked into the parking lot where people were hungrily eating their burgers and fries in their cars. He asked lots and lots of questions.

"We have a computer in Oak Brook that is designed to make real estate surveys," Kroc later wrote in his autobiography, *Grinding It Out*. "But those printouts are of no use to me. After we find a promising location, I drive around it in a car, go into the corner saloon and into the neighborhood supermarket. I mingle with the people and observe their comings and goings."

"I never viewed computers as anything more than a necessary overhead," Sam Walton wrote in his autobiography, *Made In America*. "A computer is not—and will never be—a substitute for getting out in your stores and learning what's going on. In other words, a computer can tell you down to the dime what you've sold, but it can never tell you how much you could have sold. That's why we at Wal-Mart are just absolute fanatics about our managers and buyers getting off their chairs here in Bentonville and getting out into those stores."

McDonald's and Wal-Mart use computers to tremendous effect. In fact, their business models depend on computing power. So Sam Walton and Ray Kroc were far from Luddites. They just knew when to use computing power and when to use brain power and human observational power. They knew that the essence of self-service management is to design an environment that fits like a glove; an environment the customer moves through, completing the tasks they need to complete almost without having to think.

Creating that sort of an environment requires years and years of experience, years and years of trial and error, years and years of observation of your fellow man and woman as they go about their day and seek to complete tasks. Strange as it may seem, the secret of Web success is found in psychology, not technology. That's why the Task Performance Indicator is about observing real customers—real customers attempting to complete top tasks.

RECRUITING CUSTOMERS

A typical task-measurement project involves testing 10 tasks with 15 customers. We've found that you need 15 people to test each task in order to get reliable management statistics. You can test fewer than 10 tasks but the administrative effort is such that it costs almost as much to test five tasks as to test 10. Testing more than 10 tasks means that you will be spending more time with each person. Each measurement session takes about 60 minutes, which is quite a bit of time for someone to spend testing tasks. Certainly, if the sessions go beyond 70 minutes, customers tend to get tired and frustrated, which causes them to lose concentration.

With a target of 15 customers, schedule tests with 18 because there's nearly always a few who won't turn up. Customers must be a representative mix. If you are recruiting for an intranet measurement test, for example, then here are the parameters to consider:

- **position or role in the organization;**
- **geographical location;**
- **frequency of Web site use.**

When we were testing with OECD customers, we had to factor in such things as whether they were from the public sector, private industry, media, academia, etc. We also had to factor in their roles. That is, whether they were communicators, researchers, economists, statisticians, etc. In general, we have found that job role is one of the main things you need to segment by. For example, when we were testing with Cisco we found that there were some significant differences between the tasks of technical people and those of marketing people.

Recruitment, particularly for public Web site projects, can be a time-consuming exercise. One device that has worked quite well for us is to ask people at the end of the task identification survey if they would like to participate in testing. Because of the time involved in recruiting people for testing, we recommend that you start the process as early as possible.

You don't usually need to offer incentives to recruit people if you're testing an intranet. For the testing of public Web sites, incentives are not always necessary either. However, if deemed appropriate, they can include cash, gift certificates, and freebies. Cash is the most popular and, typically, about $50 for a one-hour session is sufficient.

PREPARING THE INVITATION

When creating the invitation for people to participate, keep the following in mind:

Make the E-mail personal by using the person's name (Dear Peter Jones).

The initial E-mail should come from someone of authority that the person receiving the E-mail respects. The person sending the E-mail should state clearly who they are and what their position is.

If it's an intranet project, then, if possible, name a senior person who is sponsoring the project. If it's a public Web site project, stress that this is an opportunity for the customer to "have their say" as to how the Web site should be improved.

Briefly explain the process: That you want them to complete tasks on the Web site.

Clearly state that you are testing the Web site, not them.

Explain that you will need to record their screen and voice for later analysis and perhaps to show to some people within the organization.

Tell them that the testing will be done remotely. (If they will have to download some software in order for this to happen, let them know.) Make sure you follow up on this issue as sometimes there may be problems, particularly if the testing will occur on the customer's work computer.

If you are offering incentives, state clearly what type.

Make the invitation as short as possible. Keep it under 200 words if you can.

We go into a totally different world when we have a specific task to complete.

PREPARING THE TASK QUESTIONS

Base your task questions on top tasks, not tiny tasks. This is absolutely crucial to your success. Testing and then improving tiny tasks could actually result in higher failure rates for your top tasks. Improve the tiny tasks and you could, in fact, be moving your Web site backwards. How could that be?

- Improving the success rate of a tiny task may in fact lower the success rates of top tasks (by cluttering search results and navigation links, for example.)
- Improving the success rate of a tiny task takes time away from improving the success rates for top tasks. You are thus not maximizing the value you can deliver to your organization.
- Improving the success rates of tiny tasks will rarely show a good return on investment.

Below is a list of the top tasks we identified for the Cisco partners and OECD Web sites.

Cisco partner top tasks

1. Training and education

2. Pre-sales technical information

3. Technical support

4. Certification and specialization status, maintenance, and renewal

5. Incentive and rebate programs

6. Installation and support technical documentation

7. Product and service technical information

8. Software downloads

9. Configure a product or service solution for the purpose of quoting or ordering

10. Pricing

11. Find a product, service, or solution

OECD top tasks

1. Country surveys/reviews/reports

2. Compare country statistical data

3. Statistics on one particular topic

4. Browse a publication online for free

5. Working papers

6. Publication by topic

7. Basic facts, summaries, and overviews

8. Statistics on one particular country

9. Statistical forecasts/projections

10. Access to raw data

These are the top tasks but task questions need to be much more specific. It is pointless to ask someone to find country surveys or pre-sales technical information. You must give them a task based on a *specific* country. You must ask them to find *specific* pre-sales technical information.

This goes to the heart of task management. There is no point in evaluating Web sites in a general way, such as: "What do you think of the training section?" Never, ever trust the opinion of anyone. Observe them as they try to complete the task. You want facts, not opinions. We go into a totally different world when we have a specific task to complete. We scan webpages quickly, click links without fully reading them and don't think too much about what we are clicking and what we are scanning. But giving our opinion causes us to think about many things other than our actual behavior. Opinions about Web sites are just noise—often dangerous and misleading noise.

Cisco partner task questions

Here are some examples of task questions developed for Cisco partners.

1. Find the registration page for advanced routing and switching specialization training targeted at account managers.

2. Find a short description on how to sell Application Support multiyear service agreements.

3. Find the download page for the latest IOS software release for the 3825 NOVPN Router.

4. Find a validated design guide to help you deploy networks with 250–1,000 endpoints.

5. Your customer is saying that their 12008 router is performing very slowly. Find the guide for running diagnostics.

6. Find detailed technical specifications for the 7201 router.

7. You're selling services. Find online training on how to make sure your customers' networks are fully covered by a Cisco service agreement.

8. Obtain a report showing your company's level of certification and specialization compliance.

9. Find a datasheet describing how a Cisco security product provides malware protection and reputation monitoring as part of its E-mail and web security solution.

10. Find the list prices (in US dollars) for available mobile wireless routers.

OECD task questions

Here are some examples of task questions developed for OECD customers.

1. What are the OECD's latest recommendations regarding Japan's healthcare system?

2. In 2008, was Vietnam on the list of countries that received official development assistance?

3. Did more males per capita die of heart attacks in Canada than in France in 2004?

4. What is the latest average starting salary, in US dollars, of a primary school teacher across OECD countries?

5. What is the title of Box 1.2 on page 73 of OECD Employment Outlook 2009?

6.   Find the title of the latest working paper about improvements to New Zealand's tax system.

7.   Find a date-ordered list of Policy Briefs on the topic of employment.

8.   When were Andorra, Liechtenstein, and Monaco removed from the OECD's list of tax havens?

9.   In 2005, how much of its GDP did Austria spend on public pensions?

10. What is the predicted inflation rate, in percentage terms, for Sweden in the fourth quarter of 2010?

TASK QUESTION CHECKLIST

When developing your task questions keep the following in mind:

One unique answer

It is essential that each task has **one clear and unique answer**. Do not test tasks that have several answers because it will then be impossible to compute accurate success rates and completion times. For example:

"You're looking for training for account managers."

That's too vague. It could have several answers. Here's a more precise version:

"Find the registration page for advanced routing and switching specialization training targeted at account managers."

One task, not two

There must only be one task per question. To compute success rates, disaster rates, and completion times, there must be one task and one answer. For example:

"In 2005, how much of its GDP did Austria spend on public pensions? In 2006, did this spending increase or decrease?"

This involves two tasks:

1. Find out how much of its GDP Austria spent on public pensions in 2005

2. Find out if this spending increased or decreased in 2006

We must choose only one task:

"In 2005, how much of its GDP did Austria spend on public pensions?"

Does not contain hidden clues

Have a look at the following task:

"Find the latest working paper about improvements to New Zealand's tax system entitled 'Toward a more efficient taxation system in New Zealand'."

By including the title of the working paper, the person is given something to place in the search box. And if the search engine is any good at all it should be able to deliver a good result. So here's the task question we went with:

"Find the title of the latest working paper about improvements to New Zealand's tax system."

Uses clear, simple language

What's wrong with this task question?

"In 2005, how much of its GDP did Austria spend on public pensions?"

Does everyone understand that GDP stands for Gross Domestic Product? The audience we tested for OECD was quite professional and specific, and familiar with such terms. However, if we wanted to test the general public, we would have needed to simplify the language more.

The Cisco partners we tested were also professional and technology-oriented. Otherwise, testing the following task would not have worked:

"Find the download page for the latest IOS software release for the 3825 NOVPN Router."

Is emotionally neutral

Do not use humorous language such as puns, double-meanings, etc. Where possible, avoid anything connected with emotion. For example:

"You're feeling stressed…"

Clearly different from other tasks

There is no point in having two tasks that test whether someone can find people unless you are testing specific aspects of finding people. So, Task A might involve finding John O'Neill's telephone number, while Task B might involve finding the sales manager for Portugal.

Independent from other tasks

The completion of one task should not depend on the completion of a previous one.

Immediately doable on the Web site

Avoid a task that requires the customer to sign up and wait for verification by E-mail, for example. E-mail delivery speeds can vary substantially depending on a lot of factors, thus having unpredictable and potentially highly variable effects on the completion time.

Is not confidential

Make sure the task does not involve asking people to enter or expose personal information. To overcome such privacy issues it may be necessary, in certain situations, to create dummy accounts.

In short

Try to keep the task question nice and short as this makes it easier to understand and to act on. Keep it under 20 words if possible.

HOW THE TASK IS COMPLETED

Once you have decided on a task, you need to record the optimal way to complete it. The optimal way is the way an expert would complete the task. It involves defining and timing the navigation path that leads to an answer. Make a clear record of each step (click) in the path and take a screen grab of the answer page.

In the next chapter, we will look at how to carry out a task measurement.

chapter 15

Carrying out a task measurement

Statistical predictions are, as you would expect, fallible. But when it comes to predicting the future, human intuition — even professional intuition — is even more fallible.

David G. Myers

HOW A TEST SESSION WORKS

For each task a customer carries out you will need to measure the task completion time and make a note of key areas where they are having problems as they try to complete these tasks. Here's how a typical measurement session works:

a. **five to 10 minute introduction**

b. **roughly five minutes per task**

c. **five minutes for post-measurement interview**

Typically, within 60 minutes you will get about 10 tasks completed. Some people may complete their tasks within 30–40 minutes. Others may only complete seven or eight tasks within the allocated time. It depends on the difficulty of the tasks, the quality of the Web site and the experience of the individual customers. Always leave at least 30 minutes between tests just in case the testing goes on longer than planned.

Agree on a starting page for the tests (this is often the site's homepage). It's important that you use the same starting point for each customer. After each task, ask the customer to return to this page.

With the emergence of broadband Internet and cheap screen-sharing technology, remote testing transforms the testing environment.

WHY REMOTE TESTING IS BEST

Where possible, testing is done remotely, allowing customers to be in their own environment and on their own computer. Traditional usability testing usually involves either bringing customers to a usability lab or going to their workplace, and this approach has certain drawbacks:

1. It's more expensive and time-consuming to organize. Setting up the lab or getting to the place where the person lives or works takes time and money. It also costs the customers time and money to go to a lab. Not everyone is willing to do that.

2. One of the biggest problems with usability testing is that no matter what you say to customers, many of them still feel that you are testing them, not the Web site. Getting them to "act natural" in a lab is a lot more difficult than if they are in their own environment where there is no outside interference other than a voice over the phone.

With the emergence of broadband Internet and cheap screen-sharing technology, remote testing transforms the testing environment. It's cheaper, faster, and better because it's much less intrusive and much more likely to record natural behavior. Remote testing will lead to a revolution in task management. It will allow testing and observation to become part of our daily jobs. It will allow us to become Ray Krocs and Sam Waltons — spending most of our working week observing our customers and continuously improving the service we deliver them.

You can choose from a wide variety of software and services that allow you to remote test. Keep the following in mind:

- Make sure you know the tool well. Run several tests with colleagues before you go live. Focus on things like sharing screens, recording, and how to recover from a lost connection.
- Ideally, you should have a backup broadband option just in case one connection goes down.
- Consider using a traditional phone for communication with the customer rather than the VOIP option that most screen-sharing applications provide. Then, if the web

connection goes down, you still have telephone contact with the customer.

● Most screen-sharing services require people to download some software. Check well in advance to ensure that there are no restrictions for the customer. This can be the case particularly when you are testing someone who is at work, especially if they work for a large organization. Be prepared for the local setup of the tool on the customer's computer to take some time. Ideally, get them to install any necessary software or browser plugins in advance.

PRE-MEASUREMENT INTERVIEW CHECKLIST

Keep this initial interview under 10 minutes. Make it as informal and friendly as possible. Here's how to structure it:

1. **Introduction:** Introduce yourself and give a very brief summary of why this measurement is taking place.

2. **Permission to record:** Start recording immediately. Explain that you need to record the session and ask permission to continue. If the customer does not give permission, then stop the session. If the customer agrees, move to the next step.

3. **Test the Web site, not them:** Make it very clear that this is a test of the Web site, not them. Tell them they cannot make a mistake — that whatever they do will provide a lot of help with making the Web site better.

4. **Keep it natural:** Explain that you want them to carry out the task in the most natural way possible — as if you were not there. Tell them they don't have to explain any part of what they are doing out loud — just to go about doing it the way they normally would.

5. **Give up:** Tell the customer that if, while doing the task, they think: "I'll give up now" ask them to tell you so that you can stop the measurement.

6. **Start page:** Explain the start page that you will be using for the tests. Ask them to go to this page.

7. **Share screen:** Before you ask them to share their screen, request that they close E-mail programs or any other personal files.

8. **Any questions:** Ask if the customer has any questions before starting.

CARRYING OUT AN ACTUAL TASK MEASUREMENT

a. **Paste first task in chat box:** Paste the first task in the chat box of the screen-sharing software. Make sure the customer can see the text. Read the task aloud two or three times.

b. **Timing task start:** Ask the customer to tell you when they understand the task and to inform you when they are ready to start. Record the start time of the task.

c. **Task completion time:** When the customer believes they have completed the task, mark the end time. Make sure that they indicate the answer. It is not enough that they've found the right page; they need to specify the answer within that page.

d. **No hints:** Never give hints or in any way try to lead the customer to the answer. You may feel sorry for them as they get frustrated, but if you give them any sort of hint, you invalidate the test.

e. **Observations:** Where possible:
   a. Note each page the person clicks
   b. Note each search term the person uses
   c. Note where the customer seems to get confused or is having particular problems

f. **End of task notations:** Clearly and consistently note the following:
   a. When a task is successfully completed
   b. When the customer gives up
   c. When there is a time limit
   d. When they have a disaster (they got the wrong answer but think it's right)

g. **Task confidence:** When a customer has completed a task, ask them about their level of confidence in the answer:
   a. Completely confident in the answer
   b. Reasonably confident in the answer
   c. Not sure—I'd ask someone

h. **Five-minute time limit:** If the customer goes over five minutes, gently inform them that there is a basic time limit of five minutes. Tell them if they want to continue, no problem. Most people are only too happy to give up.

i. **Reporting:** For each task, report the following:
   a. The task description
   b. The task success rate
   c. How long it took for completed tasks
   d. Task confidence for completed tasks and disasters
   e. The failure rate
   f. The disaster rate
   g. Observations

INVALID MEASUREMENTS

Some of the reasons for invalidating a measurement are:

a. **A general technical problem occurs: For example, there are problems with the Internet connection or a computer freezes. However, if the technical problem is due to bad design or poor technical infrastructure, then it should not invalidate the measurement.**

b. **The customer misunderstands the question and tries to solve the wrong task.**

c. **The customer starts solving the wrong task and gains so much insight while doing so that the solution of the intended task is considerably influenced.**

d. **If the customer is interrupted, by a telephone call for example, for more than 10 seconds.**

e. **If the customer starts talking to you for more than 10 seconds.**

In some cases you may be able to compensate for an interruption by carefully analyzing the video recording afterwards. If you are able to determine with reasonable certainty how long the irrelevant interruption lasted, record the time the task would have taken if the interruption had not occurred.

POST-MEASUREMENT INTERVIEW

Make sure you always do the post-measurement interview. It should take less than five minutes. Use the following checklist:

a. **Which two to three things do you like most about the Web site?**

b. Which two to three things are most in need of improvement?

ETHICAL GUIDELINES

a. If, at any time, the customer says that they don't want to continue, stop the session immediately.

b. Never ask a customer to reveal sensitive, personal information. For example, the contents of their E-mail inbox, pay slips or credit card numbers. Ask them to close any windows that contain personal information before they share their screen with you.

c. Never give the customer the impression that they are doing something wrong or that they have found the "wrong" answer.

Illicit drugs and Web sites share a common language: users, traffic, and hits.

THE POWER OF OBSERVATION

It's easy to focus on the mechanics of a Web site and to base a project around producing content, buying new technology, or creating a new graphical design. They are all compelling projects that have visible results: stuff is produced, bought, and, hey, they've changed the colors. Consultants will come in and make you feel good and important. They'll talk about branding and all that jazz and it'll be fun. It won't solve your problems though.

Task management is boring and proud to be so. Task management is not about massaging your ego or your boss's. Focusing on the customer is a humbling experience; and by far the most important attribute any web team can have is the desire to serve. Customers are strangers, who don't care about you much—if at all. They're highly impatient and very ego-centric; they're all about them. But in a world where customers have more and more control, you too need to make it all about them if you are to truly succeed.

Task management is not about managing projects. It's not about managing content or technology, it's about managing tasks. Its measures are:

- **success rates**
- **disaster rates**
- **completion rates**

I guarantee you that when you start observing how your customers go about completing their top tasks, your whole view of your Web site will change. Before long you will wonder how on earth you managed before. And the truth is you didn't. Most Web sites are not managed.

As you observe your customers you will begin to notice trends; underlying reasons why failure occurs. Based on the task measurements I've completed over the years, three key areas have emerged that cause a huge number of task failures:

- **confusing menus and links;**
- **poor search results;**
- **out-of-date content.**

If you find that poor search results cause failure or significantly slow task completion in more than a quarter of the tasks measured, then you are justified in saying that your organization has a system-wide problem with search. Of course, it's not enough to report problems. Your reporting should also contain recommendations, such as: How is search going to be improved?

THE POWER OF SHOWING CUSTOMERS REAL JOURNEYS

Showing a recording of someone trying to complete a task, getting frustrated and failing is a very powerful way to communicate the need for change and improvement. The Web is a cold and distant environment and it is very hard to develop empathy for your customers. You simply don't see your customers come into your shop, store or office. You don't see their faces or hear their voices. Instead, they are "users"—one of the coldest words in the English language. These "users" are measured in hits and page impressions. (Illicit drugs and Web sites share a common language: Users, traffic, and hits.)

Presenting a recording of their journey and their strife—particularly to senior management—can have a transformative effect. The problem senior managers have with the Web is that they think it's technology; and most senior managers are secretly scared of technology. They don't understand it and feel intimidated by IT professionals speaking a foreign technical language. Anything you can do to convince management that the Web is not about technology, but rather about customers trying to do things, will benefit you and your organization.

When presenting reports or PowerPoints, try to create a series of screen grabs showing typical journeys that will illustrate why there was task failure. Again, it's all about humanizing this Web thing; taking it out of the cold climate of technology and constantly explaining that real people with real needs come to your Web site where they go on real journeys trying to click their way through to complete a top task. Take every opportunity you get to make the Web a real human environment. The more you do that, the more important the Web will become within your organization. The Web: It is really about people and tasks, not technology or content.

chapter 16

Those practical, innovative Swedes

Truth emerges more readily from error than from confusion.

Francis Bacon

By 1900, a dozen men on the floor of a mill could roll three thousand tons of steel a day, as much as a Pittsburgh mill in 1850 rolled in a year.

John Micklethwait and Adrian Wooldridge

WHAT HAPPENED TO THE NASTY NORSE?

I spend a lot of time working in the Nordic countries (Sweden, Norway, Denmark, Finland, and Iceland). As a child I grew up on tales of fierce and nasty Norsemen sailing up our Irish rivers and burning our beautiful hand-written books. (There was a time when we Irish at least claimed that ours was the land of "saints and scholars".) We were not impressed by these ignorant, book-burning, burly, big-bearded Norsemen. For a long time these Northerners loved war and general trouble-making. During the 17th century, for example, Sweden was big into picking fights, conquering its neighbors as well as many German states, and biting off big chunks of Russia and Poland.

So what happened? Instead of ravaging foreign lands, these Northerners fashioned societies that are now the envy of the world. Instead of talking about justice or praying for equality, they actually created equal and just societies. Instead of destroying things, they began to design things. They married capitalism and socialism and the odd couple seems to be getting on just fine. They gave us wonderfully-designed, affordable, truly useful products and world-class companies like IKEA, H&M, Tetra Pak and Nokia.

My good friend Fredrik Wackå and I have implemented more top task management projects in Sweden than in any other country in the world. And I have wondered what it is that particularly attracts the Swedes to the approach. Swedish design marries functionality, simplicity, and innovation. It's not about showing off or being flashy, it's about getting the job done—again and again—in the most minimal, elegant way possible. It's about function, aesthetics, affordability, and balance.

"Minimalism and practicality are virtues, and there is no shame in having the same couch as everyone else on the block," wrote Elisa Mala for *Newsweek* in 2009. "The brilliance of Swedish products is often revealed in their user-friendliness." When Swedes create a product, "they consider the person who is trying to use it," says Matthew Burger, chairperson of industrial design at Pratt Institute.

TOP TASK MANAGEMENT AT TETRA PAK

Tetra Pak has taken the concepts of top task management for an intranet further than any other organization I have worked with. I asked their E-communications director, Gabriel Olsson, why this might be. "We are both the sons of farmers," was his reply. The point he was making was that, as a farmer's son, I should understand that task management is like farming — perhaps because farmers know about the need to save time on tasks, and have been doing so longer than many industries. It's about getting the basics right and being willing to do the boring but necessary stuff (like content review) on an ongoing basis — rolling your sleeves up and focusing on what is important to your employees, not just what is cool and fun for the web team.

When a young Ruben Anderson arrived in Helsingborg from his home village of Raus, he was treated as strangers from other places often are. "What would anyone from Raus know about anything?" the other school kids chided. A lot, as it turned out, because Ruben was very smart indeed and very proud of where he came from. When Ruben became an adult he changed his name from Anderson to Rausing in tribute to his village. Sometime later, Ruben Rausing would go on to found Tetra Pak. And Tetra Pak would become a global leader in food processing equipment and packaging material, and one of the most successful global companies, through a process of continuous innovation and a relentless focus on quality.

In 2006 I was asked to help Tetra Pak review its intranet strategy. Tetra Pak followed the same intranet management models that all organizations I have worked with have followed. They had initially seen it as a technology issue and thought the key challenge was choosing the right technology with little attention being paid to the needs and habits of the employees. This approach had limited success. The other key strategic belief was that design and publishing should be distributed as much as possible. Basically, whoever wanted an intranet site and whoever wanted to publish got some training. They never kept to the use of one "right technology", as there was much freedom in the company culture and limited global planning and management. This approach, while having some benefits, had led to the classic case of the largely unmanaged and unmanageable intranet.

The Tetra Pak intranet grew, and grew fast. Nobody was quite sure how many pages there were but rough estimates of 500,000 were given. Employees were frustrated. Here are some quotes from staff:

"There is too much information today."

"I generally fail with the search engine and end up having to call people."

"I waste a lot of time trying to find information."

"I will often delay a project because I know I have to use the intranet."

"It needs to be better managed, with a more strategic approach. Time to manage!"

"If you want to be sure to lose something, post it on our intranet."

Really, you could use these quotes for any large, unwieldy intranet. The difference is that Tetra Pak actually decided they needed to do something about it. Senior management got involved and a clear vision for the intranet was established.

The intranet's number one objective is to make staff more productive.

We decided to do a top task analysis and over 800 staff (out of 20,000) voted on their top tasks. The top three task areas were:

1. Find people

2. Products

3. Procedures and policies

TASK PERFORMANCE INDICATOR AT TETRA PAK

The next step was to measure the completion of the top tasks. In 2008 we carried out extensive task measurements. The results showed that there was a lot of work to be done.

Measurement Overview

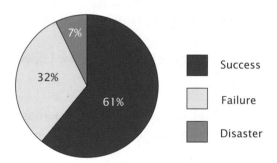

Of the tasks tested, only 61% were completed successfully; 32% of participants failed, while 7% had disasters (they got an answer they believed to be correct but which was in fact wrong).

The logic of task management is that if you are managing tasks, not content or technology, then you should measure based on task success, and that's exactly what Tetra Pak has done. The management conversation is not about getting a new content management system or search engine, or adding more intranet sites or content. It is about improving task success rates, reducing disaster rates, and improving completion times. The improvement of the task or an increase in employee productivity is the final objective, and to this end the people involved in running the intranet are called "task drivers". They drive the efficiency of the tasks and are measured on whether or not they have achieved sufficient efficiency.

As a result of measuring a wide range of tasks it became clear that there were three underlying factors that were affecting task performance regardless of the type of task:

- **confusing menus and links**
- **poor search results**
- **out-of-date information**

FIX THE BASICS

It would have been very easy for Tetra Pak to try to solve its problems by initiating some major projects to install new software and/or carry out a redesign of the Web site. It's amazing how many organizations take this knee-jerk tactical approach. The IT department gets involved and wants to solve the problem by buying new technology. Communications gets involved and wants to solve the problem by changing the graphical design.

At Tetra Pak, both Communications and IT reached a consensus. Firstly, the challenge was complex and could only be solved if both departments worked very closely together. There was a deliberate and active attempt by each department to understand each other. That was just the start of the collaborative thinking. While formal responsibility for the intranet lay within a section of Corporate Communications called E-Communications, it was quickly understood that making the intranet better would require cross-organizational support and commitment from the business.

Creating clear menus and links, improving the quality of search results, and getting rid of out-of-date content were challenges that needed to be addressed by every single person involved in publishing to the intranet. It didn't matter if they worked for Communications, Finance, or Products; or if they worked in Sweden, America, or Italy. Success would be achieved by an organizational effort. So, a lot of time was spent winning people over to the top tasks approach.

It was hard work. The motto for the new approach was: Fix the basics.

MANAGING PROCESSES, NOT PROJECTS

From all the data we have analyzed about why people are dissatisfied with their ability to complete tasks on Web sites, "confusing menus and links" is significantly ahead as the most important issue. "Poor search results" is also very significant, but "confusing menus and links" is the top issue for both intranets and public Web sites. It is the number one issue for government and commercial Web sites. It is the number one issue in the United States, Canada, the United Kingdom, Sweden, and Norway. Basically, everywhere we test, it is the number one issue.

Tetra Pak embraced the continuous improvement philosophy based on employee behavioral evidence. "Facts, not opinion" became a mantra. And that's the way the Web is going: Towards making decisions based on behavior data.

The continuous improvement model eliminates the need for big redesign projects. The project culture has often been the enemy of quality. The project itself becomes the obsession; the redesign, the graphics, the new tool. Management bonuses become contingent on the project: "implement a CMS", or "redesign the Web site", for example. There's a deadline, and that deadline must be met. Something must be launched. It doesn't really matter what — just launch something so that a box can be ticked and the higher ranks of management can be told: "Hey, look at us, we're doing stuff, we're delivering stuff. We deserve a bonus."

In Poland during the communist era there was a big office block being built. Everything was going at a leisurely pace until the local communist apparatchik arrived. Everything became frenzied as the slightly portly official in his 40s navigated a ladder and climbed up on some scaffolding. He smiled benignly as he surveyed the great speed at which his comrades were working. He chatted for some minutes with the site manager who had followed him up.

"Everyone is very busy," he said.

"The workers love being busy," came the reply.

Then the apparatchik noticed a man passing underneath with an empty barrow. He was sure he had seen the same man pass underneath him some minutes earlier with the same empty barrow. He began to track the man, observing his ant-like behavior as he scurried about the place with the empty barrow. This ant worker went here and there at great speed, but never stopped to fill the barrow. When the man came skipping underneath the scaffold again, the apparatchik shouted:

"Stop, comrade!" Man and barrow screeched to a halt. "Why don't you fill the barrow?" he asked. The poor worker's face went white and his hands began trembling like a kite fluttering in the wind.

"Too busy. Too busy to fill the barrow," was his reply, and with that he was off again, busily wheeling the empty wheelbarrow.

FIXING THOSE CONFUSING MENUS AND LINKS

Navigation design is a complex activity. It takes lots of thought and testing. It is the information architecture — the foundations —of your Web site. Get it right and everything else becomes so much easier. Get it wrong and the more content and tools you add, the more confusing your Web site will become. In other words, the more you add — the more work you do — the worse your Web site will become.

Too often, navigation design is completed in a couple of workshops, based on the opinions of the very people who should not be listened to when designing a navigation. Who are they?

The owners of content and tools. These are the worst possible people to decide what something should be called because they are too close to their content and tools. What they think is simple will be totally confusing to the typical employee. We are designing for self-service — we must vacate our brains and get inside those of our employees to see the world as they see it. Easy to say, very hard to do — but absolutely essential.

In one navigation test we did with Tetra Pak employees, the content owners said that for a particular task, employees would know to click Link A, because that's where this content had always been kept and everybody knew that. So we tested with 15 typical employees. Only one clicked Link A.

In implementing the continuous improvement model, Tetra Pak developed the following guiding principles for the navigation design:

1. Make it task based, not based on an organization, program, marketing, or tool.

2. The top task should be doable on the homepage.

3. The top five to 10 tasks should be immediately obvious from the homepage.

4. Have a maximum of 10 link options in any one navigation set. In exceptional circumstances you might go to 15.

5. Do not lay out navigation alphabetically. Put the top task first, the next task second, etc.

6. Simplify the navigational choices throughout the task. When someone clicks a classification link in the navigation, the page they go to should prominently present the sub-classes for that classification. Eliminate

all other classification options if at all possible. Remember, simplifying means taking away.

7. Make sure that the top tasks are as high up in the architecture as possible. Tetra Pak set the following objective: "Top 30 tasks must be available within one to two clicks".

8. Use continuous testing to build the navigation.

9. Do not simply focus on the homepage, or second-level pages. Think about the entire task journey instead.

10. Ask for as little effort from the employee as possible. If the task can be completed without requiring them to log in, all the better.

Think of the top level of your classification as the foundations of a large office building; it's important to get it right. So, we started with the top task data and the results from the task performance indicator, which gave us a lot of insight as to the types of links that were causing task failure or slowing down completion times. Based on this data, we delivered the first iteration of the top-level navigation:

DESIGN A

Home | About Tetra Pak | About You | Products & Sales | Technical | Processes | Collaboration

Next, we did a simplified version of the task performance indicator. We took the top task questions. Questions like the following:

How many packages per hour can the TBA19 filling machine produce?

We agreed on where we expected the employees to click, gave these top task questions to a representative sample of employees, showed them Design A and asked them:

Where would you click first to complete this task?

The data quickly illustrated that there were flaws with our initial design, with Design A having only a 60% success rate. We measured success based on whether people clicked the links we expected them to.

Have a look at Design A again:

Home | About Tetra Pak | About You | Products & Sales | Technical | Processes | Collaboration

Design A contains classic flaws of navigation design. What does "Technical" mean to an engineering organization like Tetra Pak? We might as well have a classification called "Tools" or "Infinity & Beyond". It only caused confusion and annoyance. What has been noticed through much testing is that when you present people with classifications that they find illogical or too all-encompassing, they begin to lose confidence in your design.

Some specific things we discovered from this testing included:

1. People did not understand the phrase "About You". This was the classification under which we wanted to put things like training, job vacancies, pay, etc. We did a mini-test between "About You" and "About Me", and "About Me" had much higher success rates. It is critical that good intranet navigation "speaks" to people personally.

2. The classification "Collaboration" was just confusing, as was "Processes".

Based on the results and other feedback we tested the next design:

DESIGN B

Home | About Me | About Products, Marketing, & Selling | About Technical | About Procedures & Rules | About Communities | About Tetra Pak

Design B resulted in a 70% success rate, a 10% improvement. However, there was strong feedback that employees did not like having "About" before each class. Finding people is the top task on most intranets, and we had noticed in this testing and in the overall task performance indicator tests that failure rates for this particular task were quite high. Then someone had a bright idea: Why not have a "Find People" classification? Under it we could have the find people search, the organization charts, communities, and various other collaborative activities. So, we brought out the next design.

DESIGN C

Tetra Pak Home | Products | Find People | About Me | About Tetra Pak

The test results for Design C had a success rate of over 90%. Of course, this was just the start of the process. Every major level of the classification was subsequently tested in order to improve task completion success rates.

HELPFUL SEARCH RESULTS

One of the most important things Tetra Pak did was to make people responsible for task success. It was no longer enough to make an employee responsible for the content or the technology, or the search engine. The search professional appointed had to be responsible for the findability and successful completion of the top tasks.

For too long search has been neglected as a management discipline. It has been seen as a purely technological issue when in mature environments it is far more a psychological issue. The person in charge of search should first and foremost be a search-word detective, trying to figure out what exactly the customer is looking for and delivering that page as the top search result.

Tetra Pak carried out the Search Performance Indicator process. To sum up:

1. They identified the top 300 search terms.

2. They identified the correct page for each of the search terms.

3. They searched with each of the search terms.

4. They scored each search based on where the correct page appeared in the search results. If it came first it got the highest score of 42. If it appeared beyond the first page of search results it got a zero. (For an explanation of how these scores are derived, see the section "Search with the top search words" in Chapter 11.)

5. They then began a process of ensuring correct pages appeared as high up the search results as possible.

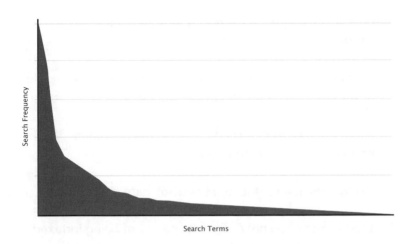

Search Terms

Tetra Pak has a search Long Neck on its intranet: A small number of search terms gets a huge number of searches.

"The situation for search was bad," admitted Gabriel Olsson. "When we started to measure, only 28% of the searches were successful." How was that score calculated? Let's say you're testing 300 search terms. The maximum score you could get would be 300 x 42 = 12,600. In other words, the correct page was first for each of the 300 search terms. So, a 28% score means that Tetra Pak got 3,528 out of a possible 12,600.

Why was search failing at Tetra Pak? Most organizations would immediately blame the search engine and a project would be set in place to buy a new one. The search engine that Tetra Pak was using did indeed have limitations but, as Gabriel pointed out, "The search application is often blamed as the only reason why search fails, and that is not the case. There is much one can fix and improve before the need for a new search engine is obvious."

A more important factor was the quality of the content. So, the next step was a rigorous review of the content environment with a particular focus on the first page of search results for each search term. What was found was:

1. Lots of duplicate and/or poorly written titles and descriptions on search results

2. Lots of pages appearing in the search results that should never have been indexed in the first place

3. Minor content that really didn't help the searcher appearing high in search results

4. Search result links that led to out-of-date content

5. The correct page not even existing or not being indexed by the search engine

Our review resulted in:

1. Rewriting content on the correct pages to increase their findability

2. Rewriting search result titles and descriptions with a focus on making sure that every title and description was unique

3. De-indexing of pages that should not have been indexed in the first place

4. Indexing for the first time of correct pages that the search engine had not been indexing

5. Creation of new pages where there was no correct page in existence for a top search term

There was also a focus on creating synonyms for the top search terms. Particular attention was paid to ensuring that no matter how you searched for a product name (TBA19, tba19, TBA 19, TBA-19) you would always get the homepage for that product as your first result.

Manual recommendations (best bets) were also used. This involved the search professional introducing into the search results a recommendation of what they thought was the best result for a particular search term.

Within six months of this effort, the success rate had moved from 28% to 57%. No new search engine, no major expenses —just a rolling up of the sleeves and a fixing of the basics. It's as old as computing: Garbage in, garbage out. Too many web teams want to build things that will help them land on the moon, when they should be sweeping the floor and washing the dishes.

Tetra Pak succeeded in improving findability because it took the Craigslist approach to web management. According to Wikipedia, Craigslist is a "centralized network of online communities, featuring free online classified advertisements — with sections devoted to jobs, housing, personals, etc.". Forty-seven million Americans visit Craigslist every month. That's more than visit eBay or Amazon.

"Craigslist does things slowly and repetitively," wrote Gary Wolf for *Wired* magazine. "Craig Newmark (who founded Craigslist) has one trait that mattered a lot in Craigslist's success. He is willing to perform the same task again and again."

Great web teams are not afraid to do the boring and repetitive; to grind out the incremental improvements. It's sexy and exciting to do the big redesign, but there is nearly always far more value — at far less cost — to be achieved by fixing the basics and adopting a day-by-day focus on the essentials.

Content creators are measured, not based on the use of the content, but rather on its production.

CONTENT QUALITY IS AS BASIC AS IT GETS

The first time I met Mats Johansson was at a workshop I was giving in Copenhagen, circa 2002. At that time Mats was responsible for the technical services and support section of the Tetra Pak intranet.

Mats believed in content quality when very few others did. It's strange that even though the Web runs on content, so few people actually care about content quality. It's as if any old content will do. Which, of course, it won't. If you want a cast iron, absolute, definitively guaranteed way to lose your employees' trust, give them inaccurate or out-of-date content. It works every single time.

When Mats worked for Tetra Pak, he would gather his intranet publishers every couple of months and go through the content they were responsible for. As part of the review process, he would show them the following slide.

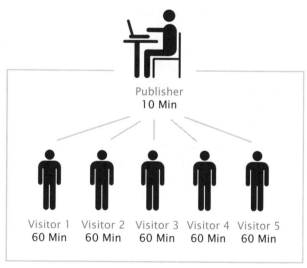

Total Time Cost = 310 Min

He explained to them that if they, the publisher, spent only 10 minutes on the content because they didn't have time to do it right, they forced the visitor (the employee) to spend 60 minutes because it was harder to find the content, harder to understand it, harder to be sure that it was correct and trustworthy. If there were five people who needed this particular piece of content for their jobs, then the overall cost to Tetra Pak was 310 minutes. And who are these visitors? They are Tetra Pak service engineers and support staff. They do important and valuable work. Their time is precious.

Then, Mats showed the publishers the next scenario.

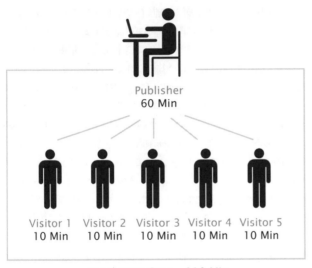

Total Time Cost = 110 Min

Let's say the publisher now spends 60 minutes on the content. Well written, clear, simple, bullet points. Good metadata, so it's easy to find. Well, now the visitor only needs to spend 10 minutes finding and understanding it. The total cost of time to Tetra Pak is 110 minutes, which is a lot less than the 310 minutes in the first scenario. And think about the potential time savings if you had 1,000 visitors! Sounds like a no-brainer that the publisher should spend more time creating quality content.

Not so. Not the way modern organizations are managed. You see, the publisher's time is measured. They work in Support or Finance or HR. The pressure is on for them to spend as little time as possible. They are not measured based on the use of the content, but rather on its production. The visitors' time is invisible. Real it may be, but it is spread throughout the organization. Nobody is responsible for it. It's not measured and we know that if it's not measured, it's not managed and if it's not managed then it cannot be important because the important things are managed.

There are other factors at work here. Often the content that is produced by a particular unit or department is for consumption by people outside that department/unit. The people working in the department don't need to read the content after they've published it because they are experts and, even if they are not, they can find an expert close by. So, they don't see the impact that poor-quality content has because they don't work with or go to lunch with the people it affects. They may genuinely think the content is simple to read. They may think it is logically organized, and it may well be excellently organized from a departmental point of view. But the classification and organizational structure that allows people to work efficiently as a team is rarely the classification that makes sense to the employee looking in.

Let me give you an example. I do a lot of workshops and talks and, thus, I prepare a lot of presentations. So, I have a folder called "Presentations" and in that folder are files called Microsoft, Cisco, Norway, etc. These file names work really well for me. Let say I'm working on a presentation for Cisco, I'll call it "Cisco". However, when the file is ready to be sent to Cisco, I'll change its name to something like "Gerry McGovern" because sending a file called "Cisco" to my Cisco contact would not be very useful for them, would it? We should never assume that a classification approach that works well for our team or department will work well for those with tasks to complete on our Web site.

SMELLY CONTENT MUST GO

You're booking into a hotel. There's a basket of fruit on the desk. You take an apple. It's a nice touch. Makes you feel welcome. It's six months later. You arrive at another hotel in the middle of nowhere. It's dark, it's late. You're tired. It's cold and raining. There are no other hotels for miles around. As you walk in the door you get hit by this truly awful smell. You struggle up to reception to see that the receptionist is wearing a gas mask. You're getting dizzy so you put your elbows on the desk to steady yourself.

Slowly, your eyes are dragged to the bottom of the desk where you see a big bowl of rotting, stinking fruit. Fungi. Blackness and yellowness. Ooze has seeped out of the bowl and slid down the mahogany in an oozy, sticky river. It's now sticking to the elbow of your jacket. You begin to faint and throw up at the same time. (You're multi-tasking.) As you fall backwards you think to yourself: "Why on earth have they left that bowl of fruit there? It must have been there for months!" But the moment just before you hit the ground, the very instant before your face hits the carpet, you think about your Web site.

Out-of-date content may not smell, but it sure does stink. It is one of the biggest Web site management problems. Nobody would leave a bowl of fruit on a desk for months, but we have no problem leaving old content on Web sites for years. Why is that? It's because the predominant culture within organizations is one of launch-and-leave. Once the content is put up, that's the job done as far as the publisher is concerned.

But unlike print content, web content never goes away. Once you publish it on your Web site, it can always be found by search engines and remains embedded in the navigation and links. Out-of-date content was not as big an issue within Tetra Pak as I have found it to be in many organizations (most intranets are glorified dumps), but it was still a pretty important factor in the poor ratings of the intranet by employees.

Elaine See, intranet program manager at Tetra Pak, used to sell online investor-relations programs to Japanese corporations. She learned a lot of quality management techniques as she met the needs of some of the most demanding customers in the world. As head of task management for the Tetra Pak intranet, she was keenly aware of the need to make sure quality standards were achieved. Supported by the content quality task driver, Elaine began to put the following strategy in place.

An initial audit was done of the whole intranet. It was estimated that there were around 500,000 pages. "No wonder you couldn't find what you were looking for," said Elaine. So, one of the first steps was to remove content published before 2006 and to set a policy in place that no more than two years of content be kept on the intranet. This sounds quite draconian but it works surprisingly well. In reality, there is very little truly old content that is of much value and where there is, exceptions can be made. By following this policy the number of pages was halved.

This was just a first step. The critical part was getting a review process in place. "On a local level there are a few units that do have regular reviews, but we need to make sure that we have a global review process to follow," Elaine told me. So Tetra Pak hired temporary staff to review every single piece of content and contact every single person who had ever published. The publishers were informed that this would not be a once-off process and that there would be a minimum of a six-monthly review cycle.

What were the review criteria? "In essence, quality content must support a task." stated Elaine. "Key questions to ask are:

1. **What does the employee need to do?**

2. **How will this content help them do what they need to do?'**

"Looking into the data, one of the key learnings is that we have a big handover issue," Elaine continued. "Employees are changing positions and companies internally, or leaving Tetra Pak, with no proper handover of intranet content. There is a lot of content 'floating around' that no longer has an owner." They began working with Human Resources to ensure that a proper handover process was put in place. The basic intent was that in the future, content without an owner would be deleted immediately. If you want to achieve quality, you need such rules and they must be followed.

CUSTOMER-CENTRIC INDEX

The first step in task management is identifying your top tasks. Then you measure their performance. It is also important to understand how people feel about their journey to complete the tasks. To this end, we have identified 13 factors that influence task completion. They are divided into three categories: Content factors; Social factors; and Information Architecture factors.

CONTENT FACTORS		
Factor	Positive	Negative
Up-to-date	Up-to-date information	Out-of-date information
Accurate	Accurate information	Inaccurate information
Complete	Complete information	Incomplete information
Language	Plain language	Full of jargon, corporate speak

For each factor we have a positive statement and a negative statement. For example, "Plain language" and "Full of jargon, corporate speak" are the positive and negative statements, respectively, for the Language factor.

SOCIAL FACTORS		
Factor	Positive	Negative
Contact	Easy to contact a person	Hard to contact a person
Participation	Easy to participate / give feedback	Hard to participate / give feedback
Open	Gives me the facts / transparent	Misleading / not transparent
Recommendations	Has ratings, reviews, recommendations	Has no ratings, reviews, recommendations

INFORMATION ARCHITECTURE FACTORS		
Factor	Positive	Negative
Search	Helpful search results	Poor search results
Menus and links	Clear menus and links	Confusing menus and links
Layout	Simple layout / easy to read	Cluttered layout / hard to read
Visual appeal	Looks attractive / appealing	Looks unattractive / unappealing
Speed	Quick to do things	Slow to do things

Participants are asked to quickly scan a randomized list of these 26 statements, and then choose the three that are most important to them.

Factor	Positive	Negative	Action
Up-to-date	6%	3%	3%
Accurate	3%	1%	0%
Complete	5%	3%	3%
Language	2%	1%	1%
Contact	5%	2%	0%
Participation	1%	2%	3%
Open	3%	3%	6%
Recommendations	1%	1%	1%
Search	5%	13%	28%
Menus and links	4%	14%	34%
Layout	6%	2%	0%
Visual appeal	4%	2%	2%
Speed	2%	7%	17%
Customer-Centric Index	46%	54%	100%

When Tetra Pak carried out the Customer-Centric Index in 2009, it received a score of 46%. In other words, 46% of the votes were for positive factors such as "up-to-date information". The above table shows that good progress has been made on the content quality front: 6% of the voters think the information is up to date, while only 3% think it's out of date. So, what are the big issues for Tetra Pak employees in completing tasks? Way out in front is "confusing menus and links" and "poor search results".

The Action column is calculated based on the size of the negative score for a factor and the gap between the negative score and the positive one. The bigger the negative score and the bigger the gap between the negative and positive scores, the higher the Action percentage will be. Think of the Action score as the customer speaking to you and saying: If you had 100 hours to make your intranet better, here's how I'd recommend you spend them. In the Tetra Pak situation, they'd like to see 34 of those "hours" spent on fixing the menus and links and 28 "hours" spent on improving the search results.

IT'S ABOUT TIME

Modern management has a blind spot. It knows how to manage workers in factories. It knows how to manage workers in offices, based on how many hours they put in and what they produce. However, it's not very good at managing "knowledge" workers. It has become very good at measuring the time that an individual knowledge worker spends, but it is very poor at measuring the productivity that results from the employee's efforts. It's easier to measure output than outcomes or impact. In the vast majority of organizations today, if an employee creates a piece of content that is not understood by its target audience, there are no consequences. There is no feedback. There is no continuous improvement of content. In a world that runs more and more on content, managers have precious little metrics to inform them if content is working or not. How do we know content is working? When it's helping people complete tasks.

Tetra Pak has started to examine how task efficiency affects productivity. In just one area it has found that improving five tasks results in a time-saving that, in money terms, corresponds to more than €125,000 per year. As another example, in the Human Resource section for Sweden they needed one less person for phone support after they introduced the task-based approach. Feedback from employees summed up the new world:

- **much easier to find than before**
- **easier to understand the information**

"Following the Task Based strategy has been the foundation of our work to successfully develop our intranet," reports Gabriel Olsson. "We have used Gary's real customer-centric approach to improve the ability of our employees to solve frequently performed tasks — in one area alone more than 50% improvement was achieved."

If we manage the publisher's time and tell them to get the content published as quickly as possible, we only think we are saving money. Maybe, in fact, we have saved money within the budget of our department. But how much money has the organization as a whole lost because our content is hard to find and hard to understand? Because it is only five minutes here and five minutes there, it doesn't seem like much time. But it all adds up to very big numbers and creates an increasing drag on organizational efficiency.

"The US economy loses millions of hours of 'citizen productivity' every year when people can't efficiently accomplish basic government tasks online," stated a white paper published by the US Federal Web Managers Council in 2008. "Agencies should be required and funded to identify their core online customer tasks, and to develop service standards and performance benchmarks for completing those tasks."

This is the big challenge and the essence of the message of this book: It's all about people's time. Time, it's all about time. And, of course, saving time is not a project, it's a never-ending journey of continuous improvement; a second here, a second there. It's also a moving target. What do employees consider to be efficient changes? We all seem to become more impatient every day and expect the same sort of effectiveness and efficiency in our company intranet experience as we get at home with the Internet and Google at our fingertips.

chapter 17

Fox meets chicken

The stock-market bubble of the 1990s coincided with an explosion in financial news.

James Surowiecki

Relying on gut feel is yesterday's strategy in retailing.

Thomas H. Davenport

Human biology has evolved as an adaptive mechanism to conditions that have largely ceased to exist.

S. L. Washburn

To say something is a product of natural selection is not to say that it is unchangeable.

Robert Wright

FOX EATS CHICKEN

Q. What do you get when you cross a fox with a chicken?
A. A fox.

The chicken is the Long Neck. The fox is the Long Tail. We need both, but we have to keep them separate. In fact, we need more than both. Organizations face three major challenges when it comes to content:

- **the chicken**
- **the fox**
- **the workhorse**

The chicken is the current content; the content you need today. It is what we think of as the Web site, the intranet. The fox is the archive, the library, the place where we store all the stuff we might need at some future date. The workhorse is the collaborative space where we work and have lots of drafts of documents and comments and ideas.

The wagons are rolling out West again into an incredibly vast, open new world. Welcome to the Content Big Bang. This is a world built on content. Think of the information you produce as the process of communicating knowledge. Your information only has value if it results in the person who receives it, acting on it. There are two ways to transfer information:

1. **Human to human interaction**

2. **Content to human interaction**

Content is information that has been recorded. We live in a world where the recording and publishing of content is exploding. A 2008 data management study by Andrew Leung at the University of California found that:

- The proportion of data that is read versus that which is created is significantly decreasing. In other words, lots and lots of stuff is created but less and less of that stuff is ever looked at again.
- Stuff is not being deleted the way it used to be. Because storage has improved, we are storing a lot more.

"Survey after survey we have done with executives indicates that the MORE organizations know about the integrity of their information management, the LESS confident they are about their ability to meet basic tests of information integrity," says John Mancini, president of AIIM, an industry association for information management.

What we also see is a rapid and inexorable shift towards the transfer of information through content to human interactions. It's self-service. People are completing more and more tasks online by interacting with content rather than other people. We live in a world where there is a management black hole when it comes to understanding the true value of quality content. This is a huge opportunity for you, a once in a lifetime opportunity. And it is all the bigger because so few people around you truly understand the implications of this shift.

GENUINE MANAGEMENT REQUIRED

This challenge will not be solved by focusing on the content itself, or on the technology that delivers the content, or on the design that surrounds the content. There is such an explosion of content that unless we bring genuine management to bear, we will all be in trouble. But what does that genuine management involve?

John Mancini recommends that executives ask the following basic management questions:

1. Is your organization able to handle the explosion of content? Does the continuing influx of content make your organization less and less effective?

2. Can your employees find content when they need it — in the daily course of business, as well as when a more urgent event or even an emergency occurs?

3. Can your employees collaborate on projects no matter where they are located in the world?

4. Has your ability to document what your organization has done, why they did it, who did it and when, gotten better or worse in the past five years?

5. Can your customers find content when they need it? Or are they abandoning your organization for a competitor who surpasses your ability to provide the information they need?

Good questions. So how can you make sure that your organization is in a position to answer them positively? By focusing on managing the tasks people need to complete, not the content, technology, or design. This book has hopefully given you some tools to identify and manage your customers' top tasks.

And you know what? If you can manage tasks, you will have a serious competitive advantage. It will truly help you to advance your career. Because you'd be amazed at the amount of people out there involved in creating and publishing content who find it extremely difficult to mentally connect content to a task.

A VILLAGE FULL OF STRANGERS

"As the media keep reminding us, the world seems as violent as ever," wrote John Horgan for *Newsweek* as 2009 neared its end. The inconvenient truth that Horgan had to point out was that "We are now living in one of the most peaceful periods since war first arose 10 or 12 millennia ago. The relative calm of our era, say scientists who study warfare in history and even prehistory, belies the popular, pessimistic notion that war is so deeply rooted in our nature that we can never abolish it."

In 2008, 25,600 combatants and civilians were killed as a direct result of armed conflicts, according to the University of Uppsala Conflict Data Program in Sweden. In the second half of the 20th century it is estimated that an average of 800,000 people a year died from war. In the blood-soaked first half of the 20th century, an average of 1.9 million people a year died as a result of war. But that was nothing to those truly savage pre-civilization societies, where an average of 25% of the population died through war. (That's 10 times the number who died through war during the 20th century.)

So why are we so afraid? It's those bloody, irrational emotions of ours; that gut instinct that tells us the world is a truly scary place. We watch TV and we think the world is in flames. Because we saw it with our own eyes. We are absolute suckers for the personal story and for the sensational event. We are extraordinarily bad at understanding data, trends, and averages.

We are now all members of Marshall McLuhan's Global Village. That means we live in a village of strangers. The Chinese, the Japanese, the Brazilians, the Americans, the Irish, the Germans, the Iranians: We're all neighbors, whether we like it or not. There are two implications:

● **greater interdependency**
● **greater need to understand the stranger**

While we're living in a Content Big Bang, we're also living through a Communication Big Contraction. With the Big Bang, everything started off as this incredibly tiny ball and then exploded outwards. With the Big Contraction the lines of communication are overlapping, interweaving, and interconnecting, and everything is being pulled together.

Every line of communication — every new Internet connection, every new mobile phone — leads to a contraction, a deepening of connections. So we're all getting closer; rubbing shoulders. We don't need to love strangers, but we do need to understand and respect them. These strangers buy our products and services. Their satisfaction underpins our future job security. This is not save-the-planet talk. It is save-yourself talk. Even the most selfish must cooperate to survive. As Richard Dawkins has pointed out in *The Selfish Gene*, "Selection has favored genes that cooperate with others."

Task management is founded on understanding the needs of strangers (your customers) and being in a constant interaction with them. It is also founded on internal collaboration and cooperation. Tasks rarely sit neatly within departments. To manage tasks is a truly cross-organizational activity. We need communications and marketing expertise, we need IT expertise, we need subject-matter expertise, and above all we need customer-service expertise. We need to bring all of that together and measure success based on the completion of the task. It's not easy to manage the tasks, but the rewards are substantial for those who do. The future is brimming with opportunity.

And we need facts, not opinion if we are to fully embrace this opportunity; continuous testing and observation of the behavior of our customers. A keen focus on what really matters: The Long Neck. And the ability to think like and use the words of our customers. To realize that our gut instinct is organizational-thinking and that to break out we must constantly interact with our customers.

As a child living on a small, isolated farm I envied those wagons going out West to find a new world and new opportunities. Not anymore. I feel truly privileged to be part of one of the greatest wagon trails in history. This Web of interconnections, interdependencies, and inter-opportunities is huge, and getting bigger. We're in the middle of the beginning of it all.

And to quote Charles Darwin in *The Descent of Man*:

As man advances in civilization, and small tribes are united into larger communities, the simplest reason would tell each individual that he ought to extend his social instincts and sympathies to all the members of the same nation, though personally unknown to him. This point being once reached, there is only an artificial barrier to prevent his sympathies extending to the men of all nations and races.

Further Reading

Ayres, Ian. *Super Crunchers: Why Thinking-by-Numbers is the New Way to Be Smart.* London: Bantam, 2007.

Beinhocker, Eric D. *Origin of Wealth: Evolution, Complexity, and Radical Remaking of Economics.* Boston: Harvard Business School Press, 2006.

de Bono, Edward. *Simplicity.* London: Penguin, 2009

Dell, Michael. *Direct From Dell: Strategies that Revolutionised an Industry.* Rev. ed. London: Profile Business, 2000.

Feynman, Richard. *Cargo Cult Science.* California: Caltech commencement address, 1974

Gladwell, Malcolm. *The Tipping Point.* Rev. ed. London: Abacus, 2001.

Goldacre, Ben. *Bad Science.* London: HarperPerennial, 2009.

Kuhn, Thomas S. *The Structure of Scientific Revolutions.* 3rd Rev. ed. Chicago: Chicago University Press, 1996.

Micklethwait, John and Adrian Wooldridge. *The Company.* Library Paperback ed. New York: Modern Library Inc, 2005.

Myers, D. G. *Intuition: Its Powers and Perils.* Rev. Ed. London: Yale University Press, 2002.

Ridley, Matt. *The Origins of Virtue: Human Instincts and the Evolution of Cooperation.* London: Penguin, 1998.

Surowiecki, James. *The Wisdom of Crowds.* Rev. ed. London: Abacus, 2005.

Taleb, Nassime Nicholas. *Fooled by Randomness: The Hidden Role of Chance in Life and in the Markets.* 2nd ed. London: Random House, 2005.

Wilson, T. D. *Strangers to Ourselves: Discovering the Adaptive Unconscious.* Boston: Harvard University Press, 2004

Wright, Robert. *The Moral Animal.* Rev. ed. London: Abacus, 2004.

Index

Index